Historical Mysteries of Wakefield

P.A.Ross

Copyright © 2019 P.A.Ross

All rights reserved.

ISBN: 9781072215172

DEDICATION

For my beautiful Granddaughter, Sinead

CONTENTS

	Acknowledgments	i
1	Foreword	1
2	The Beginning	Pg 8
3	Wakefield's First Occupants	Pg 13
4	The Romans	Pg 17
5	Saxons & Vikings	Pg 29
6	The Normans	Pg 36
7	Two Castles	Pg 38
8	The battle of Wakefield, 1460	Pg 49
9	An unknown Castle, An unknown battle	Pg 57
10	Tunnels	Pg 91
11	A lost tower	Pg 97
12	The origins of the Bullring	Pg 101
13	Battlefield bodies	Pg 103
14	Missing monuments	Pg 112
15	A lost Hermitage	Pg 116

ACKNOWLEDGMENTS

I would like to thank the Admin and members of the Facebook groups, Waccanfeld and Yorkshire Historic Group with a special thank you to Cliff Jones and Jon Holey for the help with my research and for giving me someone to bounce ideas off. The following book was only possible thanks to the following people, Associations and Websites J.W. Walker, Benjamin Clarkson, John Goodchild, The Yorkshire Archaeological & Historical Society, The Portable Antiquities Scheme, English Heritage, British Museum, The St John's Museum, Google Earth, Spectrum Spacial Analyst, Lidar Finder, Academia.eu, Magic Map, Archi UK, West Yorkshire Archaeology Advisory Service, Anthropological Studies Center.

1 FOREWORD

"You must always be willing to truly consider evidence that contradicts your beliefs, and admit the possibility that you may be wrong.

Intelligence is not about knowing everything; it's the ability to challenge everything we know."

I am not sure who the above quote was originally said or written by, I found it on Facebook and felt it was a good opener for this particular book.

In my previous history book about the city of Wakefield, I covered many historical periods and quite a lot of the historical people and the events which took place in or around the City.

Although the majority of the "A History of Wakefield" book was correct it did prove that even when you think you have the full story or the correct one, what you may read or the information you discover is not necessarily the truth.

There were a couple of inaccuracies in the first edition of my previous book which I have since amended.

In the information about Lofthouse I stated that Lofthouse Park was the world's "First" theme park.

This is incorrect as Blackpool pleasure beach predates Lofthouse and the Black gang Chine on the Isle of Wight predated both Blackpool and Lofthouse Park.

I was also incorrect about part of the information in regards to Horbury Castle, the river there does not form a natural oxbow, the oxbow was created when the canals were built, however I still stand firm on my theory of where the castle was situated.

As much of what we know about history was written by those with money and education, in a time when few had this privilege, and the technology of the time did not give us the information it can today, it has to be said that not all that is written by early historians can be taken at face value.

What I am referring to here is that much like this book, historians such as J.W Walker and Benjamin Clarkson used their own theories in their writing, these theories were not unfounded and uneducated guesses they were based on the groundwork, knowledge and information available to them at the time.

As such we cannot ignore their information but we can use it as a guideline, querying it as we search and gathering our own research.

Since the advancements in technology over the last thirty or so years there have been many new and fascinating discoveries in the world of archaeology all across the world, a rise in metal detecting clubs has given us access to information previously lost, in the last year alone (2018) there were three hordes of coins discovered in the area by just one local club.

Even a small city like Wakefield has had its fair share of recent discoveries such as the tanneries beneath the new courthouse on Westgate and Roman Roads at Snow Hill Retail Park.

These new discoveries and the information that they can provide, tell us much more than the history books written in the 18th, 19th and early 20th Centuries can, the tendency to "romanticize" the past by the authors of those times has clouded the minds of many with more than a passing interest in history.

Historical timelines tend to be set around the seat of whichever royal figure was on the throne at the time, and these books also focus majorly on the elite and their roles in history often ignoring the common man and woman and their roles in the shaping of this great country.

This is now changing and along with technological advances like Lidar (ground penetrating radar), satellite mapping and geophysics studies, we know more about how the commoner lived in the past and it has opened up new questions as well as many new theories on history in general.

This book is based on my own personal theories using my experience and the tools at my disposal to uncover some of the History Mysteries surrounding Wakefield, questions I have asked myself and those which have been asked by people on the many Facebook groups celebrating the history of Wakefield and Yorkshire.

I decided it was time that a new theory of history mysteries and the story of Wakefield through the ages was to be released upon the public, although some of this information may not have a conclusion to it, the information has been researched to the best of my abilities.

Before we begin the story of Wakefield, I wanted to answer a question that I am often asked, what information do I use when working on my historical theories and how do I come to a conclusive decision in regards to a period or event in history?

Like many researchers my main tool is the internet, there are many websites, social media groups and forums available packed with information, old maps and scans of historical documentation many complete with translations.

The problem with using forums, Wikipedia and some websites is the information provided there is often the same information within the early history books or it is often incorrect so I will always check with several sources.

Other major tools are the Archaeological reports, these hold information in great detail about all of the archaeological digs which have taken place, in the last thirty or so years across the country.

Much of this information is available online to anyone with the knowledge and relevant computer skills to find it.

I have studied archaeological techniques from detailed reference books and gathered information from those with more experience in this field than I, some of the main skills I have gained are, knowing how to read the landscape, recognizing artefacts and identifying historical locations which may be of interest or importance.

I spend hours upon hours searching and comparing many old maps with the modern landscape, I use Google Earth and Lidar mapping tools, information from official sources such as the British Museum, the Yorkshire Archaeological services and the Portable Antiquities Scheme.

Along with the internet sources there are also other areas I will pursue to gather information, as mentioned in my previous book I have a keen interest in metal detecting, I understand the importance of field walking and the logging and reporting of finds.

I use common sense and take a realistic outlook and I have the ability to separate fact from fiction, these are just a few of the weapons in my arsenal of tools, I also have over 40 years of studying and learning about history, as such I have a good understanding of many different periods.

With these tools at my disposal I am able to piece together the stories and like any good historical detective, determine the most likely path history took based on dates of finds, corresponding with information gathered from the above tool box.

Fieldwork is more important than information gathered online and most of the time I will visit a location to see it with my own eyes as it is too easy at times to misinterpret the information we read.

It is also noteworthy to point out that mistakes are made (as already mentioned I have done this myself in the past) information gathered by pre mid-20th Century antiquarians and historians may not be the entire truth and only based on the information they had at their disposal at the time of writing, without getting our feet on the ground we are basing our theories purely on those who came before and retelling stories already told.

I prefer to tell the story of history that is unknown or that which will help to rewrite history as we know it.

History is like a jigsaw puzzle where many of the pieces are missing or have been turned upside down showing only their underside, but using the tools available and with the technological advancements in archaeology and research, we are able to build a new picture of our history.

I am now going to tell you the story of Wakefield, from the beginning. This is purely theoretical yet it is based on information gathered using the above skills and sources.

Like many history books, the words within this volume are not meant to be taken as the "Gospel", I do believe that the following is a great possibility of how Wakefield became the City rich with history that it is today and as such we will begin at the beginning.

2 THE BEGINNING

Long before human occupation of the valley where Wakefield now stands proud upon a hill overlooking the River, the land was a tropical paradise with many species of tropical plants and fauna growing, providing food for the dinosaurs which are said to have roamed this part of Yorkshire.

Omnivores would have once wandered across the land providing food for much larger predators, the carnivores of the time.

It is possible that the Tyrannosaurus may have hunted Anklyosauria in the tropical haven which once stood here, although no official evidence has been discovered of dinosaurs in or around Wakefield (the closest was the Anklyosauria discovered near Harrogate) it has to be presumed that these creatures did wander around this location too as remains of prehistoric fish were discovered on Westgate during building work thus proving that there was life in the vicinity during this era.

At this time Britain was not an island, we were just a piece of land connected with the land that would become Europe, We cannot say exactly how the landscape looked at this time but from archaeological evidence gathered across the country it suggests that there may have been volcano's, deep lakes and masses of jungle-like woodland covered in tropical plant fauna and we do know for certain that the creatures, such as those mentioned above, did roam this part of the land.

We are told that the Ice Age was responsible for the wiping out of the dinosaur population, and with it the landscape and topography of the world including the land that would become the City of Wakefield, all changed dramatically and as the Ice melted it left scars upon the landscape, shaping mountains and valleys, river beds and streams, all across the land which would become Great Britain.

Some of these scars can still be seen today using Google Earth, they appear as tree branches in the earth spanning in all series of lengths and directions.

Indeed "Gods Own County" Yorkshire, was born around this time and although it would not become known as Yorkshire for a long time to come, this beautiful, inspiring landscape of winding valleys nestling among green forest covered hills with stunning waterfalls, rugged hills and vistas of mind blowing proportion was formed.

The countryside which would inspire future poets, authors and artists to create everlasting pieces that would put Yorkshire on the map.

In Wakefield the receding and melting ice created several natural hills and rocky outcrops and with it the River Calder, the major high points in Wakefield being where the Cathedral now stands, Heath Common, Lindale Hill, Lowe Hill, Sandal castle hill, Eastmoor, Lupset and Outwood.

The whole area became covered in thick oak and birch trees, it was a woodland which would cover the length and breadth of the country and become home to packs of wolves, droves of deer, bears, lions and wild hogs who all occupied the dense forest.

Beneath the ground the rich Layers of Iron ore, deep Coal seams and layer upon layer of Sandstone were formed in great masses, making Wakefield an ideal location for future settlers (and a future hub for industrial activity), everything was laid out like a tapestry awaiting man to come along and take advantage, which of course they did.

Beside the River Calder areas of swampy marshland appeared, fed by the overflowing bank of the river. Where the estate of Flanshaw now stands would have been nothing but waterlogged marsh covered in bulrushes and reeds with a couple of hills poking through, this sight would have been repeated in many of the low lying areas of the city including where the Pugneys water park now stands.

In the warmer months the river would have been much lower providing crossing points in several places where one could wade or paddle across to the far side, the most well-known of these is where the Chantry Chapel bridge now stands and recently in 2019 the river was so low that the original crossing could be seen clearly running beside the Chantry bridge in the direction of the chapel.

Now it is just piles of small rounded pebbles and a few larger rocks and as I gazed down from the wall of Chantry Bridge, I could imagine what the painter of one of my favorite paintings of Wakefield had seen when he created his piece, the picture depicting the river crossing, with cattle being driven through the water and across the ford, in the foreground there were people washing their clothes on the banks of the river.

This painting was a very large piece in oils by an artist whose name escapes me, it hung proudly in place in the old Wakefield Art Gallery on Wentworth Street, sadly now closed, I have not visited the newly built Hepworth Gallery (Wentworth Street's replacement) to see if this particular painting is still displayed, I hope it is as it gives the viewer a rare insight into the past at one of Wakefield's most famous sites.

It is not known when people first began using these crossings but we do know that there was a route from Chester to Leeds which ran through Gawthorpe in Ossett and as such there must have been a crossing in use leading up to this causeway.

I believe that Chantry Bridge and the footbridge at Horbury leading towards Broadcut Lane, are the only two remaining crossing places still in use that predate where many of the modern bridges now cross, although today your feet would stay much dryer than before the bridges were built.

3 WAKEFIELD'S FIRST OCCUPANTS

This new landscape soon brought with it human habitation, it is said that nomads from Africa travelled into Europe and across Doggerland the ancient piece of land connecting Britain to mainland Europe, to settle in Britain.

It is a possibility that they were following migrating animals or perhaps they were just following their feet? Eventually they settled down on this land.

The ancient highway at Gawthorpe leading from Chester to Leeds and the Stone Age axes found at Lindale Hill tell us that people were at least passing through this area or maybe hunting here as early as the Megalithic and Mesolithic periods however there is very little evidence to say that early man settled here.

It is more likely that Stone Age man hunted in the area and did not stop for any longer than it would take to stalk his prey, kill it and skin it before moving on.

The first settlers in the Wakefield area were here sometime around the Bronze Age, we find people were buried on land around Mitchell Laithes farm at Earlsheaton near Ossett and a Henge stood at Birkwood near Altofts and there is also evidence of hunting or forestry in the form of a hoard of bronze axes discovered at Stanley Ferry.

It is unknown at the time of writing this book, if there are any other Bronze Age sites around the Wakefield area but this isn't to say that there was no other activity in and around the locality.

We have the evidence of bell pits, which have been used since early man discovered flint, and these are evident right across the Wakefield district, the largest collection being on the south side of Wakefield near Bretton.

Although some of these have been identified as being Medieval in origin there are areas that have not been investigated thoroughly such as fields containing bell pits off Ouchthorpe Lane, and the Iron Age related bell pits at Dogloich woods in Gawthorpe.

It would appear that the mining of ore and coal took place in and around Gawthorpe and

Kirkhamgate from the Iron Age onwards, the thick coal and iron ore seams which run beneath these two small villages also contain many fresh water springs travelling through them, the thick forest would have supplied all the food and wood they required to live as comfortably as one could in this particular period and nearby clay beds at Wrenthorpe would have provided the materials to make pots for cooking.

I was informed that an archaeological dig did take place somewhere to the rear (north) of Dogloich Woods and at least two round houses were discovered, I have been unable to find a copy of the dig report as yet but with this information we can safely say that there was a settlement of sorts there.

This area seems to have been a central hub for the production of Iron ore right through to the Medieval period, there was an iron workings along the river Chald (the small stream which runs into the Calder from a spring in Gawthorpe via Flanshaw) this site was situated only a few hundred yards from the bell pits and the area was riddled with pig iron deposits, the evidence we have of this area all points to the occupation, production of and possible trading of iron ore and iron tools, passing throughout the ages.

Other Iron Age identified sites include a location off California Drive at Whitwood which was identified as an enclosure, possibly a small settlement or farmstead however there is little information about this site to go by and I believe it may have been covered over with modern buildings now.

It is alleged that there may have been an Iron Age fort on or close to Lupset golf course, below "The Mount" and situated in a small woodland to the west of the school , however I don't believe there was any substantial evidence to prove this theory and this is a location that requires further investigation by professional archaeologists.

There are no more Iron Age sites that we currently known of around Wakefield, however it is my theory that the site between Gawthorpe and Kirkhamgate did not just disappear into thin air but flourished through the years providing iron ore and ingots or goods to whomever would purchase them.

This would include foreign invaders and although there is no evidence of the Romans to be found in the city, other than one or two single coins which may have been lost by a small patrol from the large settlement at Castleford, or perhaps they were dropped by someone hunting in the forest which covered the hill where the Cathedral now stands, these are the only proof of any activity in the Centre of Wakefield during the Roman occupation.

4 THE ROMANS

We are told that there were at least four Roman roads travelling through Wakefield, one of these follows Doncaster Road where an alleged "Aggar" (Roman Banking) stands below Heath Common, now overgrown with bracken, ferns and blackberry bushes it is difficult to pinpoint from the ground unless a person knows what it is they are looking at, but can be seen on Google Earth quite clearly as a banking running parallel with the A638 towards Wakefield.

Two more Roman roads were recently discovered in the area surrounding the newly built Snow Hill Retail Park and according to J.W. Walker there is another Roman Road which is said to have run close to Lowe hill and in the direction of Snapethorpe perhaps a continuation of the road by the A639 Doncaster Road.

With this said there have been no Roman military artefacts discovered in or around Wakefield and the only evidence of settlement dates to sometime in the last 70 years of the Roman occupancy of Britain and even this is sketchy and debated.

Was there a villa at Snapethorpe?

J.W. Walker received his information about the villa from a man called William Briggs who occupied land in Thornes, he told Mr. Walker that as a young boy he had seen some Roman tessellated Pavements beneath the field between Ossett StreetSide and Snapethorpe Hall, this information was corroborated by Mr. Benjamin Milner who's Knowledge of it went back 70 years.

We have to ask was Walker's information correct? After all, the information was given to him by two men, one of which had been a child when he saw the alleged tessellation.

It is safe to say that in this time (19th Century) when both men claim to have known about it, that they would have more than likely had no clue as to what was Roman and what was Georgian in design, for either of them to be able to recognize Roman tessellation as being legitimate would have taken more than a passing knowledge of the Romans and for a child to know the difference especially in this period would have been very doubtful.

In this time there had been few Roman sites uncovered so for either men to have been able to recognize the find and date it as Roman is highly unlikely unless they had visited one of the few identified sites with similar tiles, but again to the untrained eye one piece of tile is as old as another.

Even today it would be easy for the uneducated eye to mistake a piece of Roman tile for a modern one and to identify it to a specific period it would take years of research and a good knowledge of recognizing artefacts from that period.

Information has arisen since then that a "Master Robert Carpenter paid 2s rent for his house (villa) at Snapethorp" which I believe is from the court manor roles of 1342 perhaps this is the villa referred to?

The word Villa has meant a large house since the Roman period and it has never ceased to represent this, as such we have to ask is the term Villa associated with Snapethorpe, just a simple word for large house of any period?

This account in the court roles however, was 932 years after the Roman's left Britain so it would be doubtful to have been of Roman origin although we do know some Roman architecture does survive the test of time so perhaps this was a Roman villa renovated and reused all those years later or it was a building simply referred to as a villa.

Personally I believe that this wasn't a Roman site but a large house dated to the 14th Century possibly even the predecessor to Snapethorpe Hall which was built either on or close to the site, it is debated as to whether the villa itself was beneath the footprint of the later hall or if it was situated beneath Snapethorpe school.

However reports of Roman tiles do appear in information related to the demolition of Snapethorpe Hall, and it is understandable that there is some confusion regarding its precise location.

A site which was confirmed to be of the Roman period was discovered in Alverthorpe during the building of houses on Highfield Drive and at the location of an old quarry, the Archaeological report details the discovery of under floor heating tiles, the archaeologists also discovered a very rare Armchair Voussoir which is an unusual vaulted style archway used in Roman bath-houses and one of only a few ever found in Great Britain.

Roman marching camps were alleged to be in the vicinity, at Lofthouse and at Kirkhamgate, the one at Lofthouse I have since proved not to be of Roman origin but dated to the 12th Century onward (the full report of this can be found in my book A History Of Wakefield) and the site at Kirkhamgate has not provided any Military finds to date however it did yield 5 Roman coins in recent searches of the land by two friends that I took to the site to metal detect, with permission of the land owner.

It is my theory that the Romans did not invade Wakefield, there was technically nothing here to invade other than a few small settlements scattered around the outskirts of the woodland covered hill, settlements which could provide useful resources without using Roman manpower.

It is known that many Britons were romanized throughout the 367 year occupation of the Roman's in Britain and it is more than possible that this was the case with the few settlements around Wakefield, did they adopt the Roman way of life just as many other settlements, towns and villages did throughout England? Did they accept their beliefs, wear their clothing and hair styles and use their techniques for production?

By the time the artefacts found at Alverthorpe would have been made, the Roman empire had become Christian and as such this religion became more visible in Britain although many Britons held firm to their "Pagan" beliefs some did adapt.

But what about the Roman coins which were found at Kirkhamgate and other locations? The Coin molds discovered at Lingwell Gate? Not to mention the Roman roads and other Roman artefacts people have found in the Wakefield area?

Surely the discovery of these artefacts means that the Romans were here?

The short answer to this is yes, the Romans were here but not specifically in person, more than likely it was their customs, beliefs, techniques and monetary system that invaded Wakefield and not Roman soldiers or Roman born civilians.

The Romans may have only been visitors in the area, using the roads that have been discovered to travel from Castleford to their forts in the West or hunting for food among the great oaks, the coins discovered at Kirkhamgate and Stanley were all dated to the latter end of the occupancy so is it possible these were for payment of goods?

Perhaps the site at Kirkhamgate/Gawthorpe provided the Iron the Romans required in Castleford? We shall explore this more later in this chapter, for now though I would like to focus on the site at Alverthorpe which I am unsure of, it appears that it could have been a Bath-house, however the location of a nearby quarry pit and kilns would say to me that this was possibly the home of a rich potter or perhaps a stonemason especially with the information below.

Evidence of this site is quoted by Leatham (1845, p. I08) in an extract from a lecture given to the Wakefield Mechanics Institute in 1842;

"We are informed that Roman coins and urns have been dug up at Alverthorpe very nearly in line with the Roman Road."

Roman coin molds were also discovered during the widening of a brook in Alverthorpe (Boyne 1855 pp 41-4).

Many small fragments of sandstone were discovered around the quarry site, including some "which look" to have been burnt and discolored, it "appeared" that the material had been thrown into a pit deliberately, "possibly" the remains of stone masonry taking place?

Remnants of "Romano-British" pottery and tile fragments were also found along with burnt stone, coal and charcoal "suggesting" that this was a rubbish pit where the ashes from a fire along with broken pottery and tiles were thrown, this again "suggests" the activity of production on the site "perhaps" these were the remnants of inferior items that did not form correctly or cracked in the kiln?

The finds from this site were dated from the 2nd to the 3rd century suggesting that manufacturing was occurring on this site before Kirkhamgate was possibly involved with the Romans, the coins discovered at Kirkhamgate dated to the 4th Century so it is possible that trading did not commence until much later than the site at Alverthorpe or maybe manufacturing stopped in the 3rd century at Alverthorpe?

Perhaps it took longer to persuade the locals to trade or conform to the customs and ways of life that the Romans lived? Or perhaps the site at

Kirkhamgate/Gawthorpe was abandoned for a while before being brought back to life around 350 AD.

The suggestion of Batley Road being of Roman origin has no physical evidence to back it up but it does pass the site at Alverthorpe and runs very close to the location a large amount of Roman coins were found at Kirkhamgate which is only a short distance from the Iron works, so it would appear plausible to anyone that this was a Roman road.

However as you have probably gathered this book is not about just putting pieces of the historical puzzle together, it is about looking deeper into the information we have about specific periods.

We know from written accounts which have been translated, that the Romanization of Britain took place, we know that their coinage was in use by just about everyone within the first 100 years of occupancy until their departure.

We know that Britons learned the Roman techniques for finer pottery, metal working and architecture and adopted these as a way of life, although it has to be repeated that not all Britons took this laying down and some never accepted the change.

The more recent Roman period discoveries at Snow Hill I have yet to read the archaeological reports fully for, but I can presume that they will have physical evidence for these as that is the practice in this day and age and it will be exciting to see how these roads fit into the modern landscape and with the story of Wakefield and the Roman period.

So if they were, why were the Romans trading with locals around here? We know that there are coal seams at Glasshoughton which is just up the road from Castleford, but what about Iron ore?

I discovered that there are beds of ironstone beneath Castleford and in locations much closer than Wakefield, so it seems implausible that they would require Iron from a site so far away. So how did the coins end up at Kirkhamgate?

By the 4th Century Roman coinage was the common currency throughout the Roman Empire and this included England and of course Wakefield.

Everyone would have been using the system of coins to pay for goods, even if the residents of Kirkhamgate were not selling their iron to the Romans it would make sense that they probably made a good amount of money from the operation of the mines and bell pits in the area which would give them a large amount of Roman coins.

How they ended up buried in what would become a cow grazing field years later, we may never know.

This may be disappointing to many, as it is

interesting and perhaps a little exciting to imagine that the infamous and powerful Roman army may have once walked this land, after all their invasion of Britain is as much a part of Wakefield's history as any other town, village or city in England, however evidence points to the fact that no Roman army settled in Wakefield and they only passed through to build roads or perhaps trade, hunt or fish and it is more than likely that no one of Roman origin settled here either.

When I first began researching the Romans in Wakefield I had many theories mostly based on an overactive imagination or far strung possibilities which I had to explore, one of these was the theory that the alleged marching camp at Kirkhamgate was a stopping off point for a retreating army, possibly from one of the Forts on Hadrian's Wall.

This goes to show how research actually works, we follow one lead, which may in turn lead to something else, new information comes to light, often we end up returning to our original lead and dismissing where it took us as you will see from the following, but when a theory or lead gives us new questions or even answers, then that is what makes researching and discovering history so exciting.

I followed this theory for a while drawing lines from each of the 16 forts to the farthest fort in the south of England at Lympne on the south coast, in doing so I was surprised to see one of these lines (from Vindolanda the most famous of all) ran exactly through the site at Kirkhamgate.

Could I be correct? Further research proved me to be very much wrong, I was corrected by a friend on the evacuation point of the Roman army, it was in fact Colchester where they departed, I also discovered that the military occupation of Hadrian's wall was a slow decline and not a large military operation, the soldiers and their families leaving in small groups throughout the latter 70 years or more of the occupation

I re-drew the lines from each of the walls fort's and this time not one passed even close to Wakefield and so, with these facts, and the lack of Military finds at either of the alleged "marching camps", it is my conclusion that the closest the Roman army got to settling in Wakefield (other than to build roads or pass through) was at Castleford.

No matter which way we look at it there is no substantial proof that any person of Roman origin lived in or on the outskirts of Wakefield.

The majority of archaeological reports that refer to the Romans in this area tend to use words and lines such as:

"Thought to be of Roman origin"

"Could be Romano-British"

"Seems to be of the Roman period"

"Looks similar to other Roman sites"

Etc... Whilst also referring to most of the finds as Romano-British and not "Roman".

It has to be said though that the Roman army did not just consist of those from Italy, it was built upon volunteers and slaves from all corners of the Empire and as such without discovering dateable and location identifiable human remains from this period and/or masonry with Roman inscriptions, we may never know if any Roman lived in Wakefield.

If indeed the Romans had settled in Wakefield we would have discovered Roman Burial grounds, Temples and more than one Bath-house, there would be stonework with Roman script carved into it, military objects relating to the great Roman army, all of which have been discovered in other places of Roman origin in England but not in or around Wakefield.

5 SAXONS & VIKINGS

The departure of the Romans in 410 AD left Britain in a state of panic; invaders from Saxony set their eyes on this small island.

At least this is what we are taught, to date there have been no Saxon battlefield sites discovered in England despite extensive searches by archaeologists and historians, and very little is known of the period between 410 and 600 AD, there are very few written works surviving from this period and those which do are very fragile manuscripts, and although these have been translated by experts, sometimes things do get lost in translation and what we are told is not necessarily what was written.

Did the Saxon's invade? Or did they arrive peacefully and integrate with the Britons? Some modern historians believe that the Saxon's did not actually invade England but settled here as immigrants coming over in small groups and not a large army as suggested.

It is thought that Horbury castle was of Saxon origin as is the church in the village so perhaps at this time Horbury was the largest settlement closest to Wakefield.

An Anglo-Saxon cross dated to the 9th Century, was discovered beneath the cathedral, remains of which now stand in Wakefield museum proving that the hill was a site of worship for many years.

In 2016 a beautiful modern replica of this cross was placed on a site outside the Cathedral's west doors to mark its recommitment to the people of the city and region and the end of its refurbishment project.

But why did they choose this place to worship? Was it the locality of the springs? Or perhaps it was the abundance of wildlife and woodland? What made the hill of Wakefield so special and holy to those who believed?

Fresh water springs were seen to be holy places as far back as the Bronze Age with people throwing sacrificial offerings into them to please the God's and Wakefield is full of natural springs which may have been the reason for a settlement to grow here.

It would make sense that a location such as the hill would be chosen for worship.

The Romans are known to have been responsible for clearing much of the woodland in Britain and sometime between their departure and the arrival of the Vikings in Northumbria in 793 AD the woodland which covered the hill is thought to have been cleared and the cross was erected at sometime around 800 AD.

Although the following location is not in the immediate vicinity of the city, the Saxons did have another connection to Wakefield.

The battle of Winwaed was the definitive battle between Christianity and Paganism fought on the 15th November 655, the last pagan King, Penda, was killed here along with several other pagan nobles and it is said to have possibly taken place at the great north road crossing of the River Went at Wentbridge, it is also proposed that the Christian army of Osric made camp prior to the battle, on the site now occupied by Nostell Priory.

Very few Saxon finds have been discovered in Wakefield and it seems that there was very little activity around here until long after the Viking invasion; it would appear that the cross may be related more to a Christianized Viking or Anglo-Saxon if in fact Wakefield is named after a person called Wacca.

The Vikings are also a people who seem to be scarce around Wakefield, the "alleged" Viking

Longboat discovered at Bottom Boat seems to be the only Viking era discovery ever found and even this does not seem to be Viking craftsmanship or design and so it is my theory that this boat was built in the correct period but by a local Anglo Saxon and not a Viking.

Wakefield has many Viking themed place names, Lupset, Ossett, Kirkthorpe, Chapelthorpe, Kettlethorpe, Alverthorpe, Humble Jumble bridge and other locations which give us the impression that they played a large part in the discovery of Wakefield, yet if this were the case surely there would be more evidence of their existence?

Unlike York, where they have discovered dwellings, artefacts and documentation to prove that the Vikings were there, Wakefield has no archaeological evidence and no written evidence to prove that the Vikings even stepped foot in the area even though it did come under their Dane-law.

There are many theories of how Wakefield got its name, however in the Domesday Book of 1086 it is named as Wachfield and held a population of 9 villagers, 22 smallholders, 11 freemen and 3 priests proving that a settlement had been established here before the book was written.

So what happened in Wakefield between the Viking invasion in 793 and the Norman invasion of 1066? With the name Wachfield it is doubtful that the origin of the name came from a person called

Wacca, even though we know that the English language has changed dramatically throughout the centuries.

My personal theory is that if we break the word into two we get Wach Field, perhaps "Wach" is a misspelling of the word Watch? Or perhaps this is the correct spelling of the word at the time of writing, after all the English written language did not become recognizable as we know it today until the late 19th Century.

Wakefield has several outcropping natural hills making it a perfect location for watching over the crossing of the River Calder.

Is it possible that Wakefield derived from the words Watch Field, meaning a location guarding a particular point of interest, a field to watch from?

The Castle at Horbury seems to predate any settlement at Wakefield so perhaps Watch Field was associated with the castle there, a field to keep watch over the crossing further upstream where Chantry Bridge now stands only a few miles from the castle? Or perhaps it was a place for farmers to watch over their cattle as they drank from the river.

Could it be that Wakefield was an outpost of Horbury castle?

What is known about the Saxons and Vikings in Wakefield is that there is no actual evidence proving either of these people lived in or close to the city Centre, although the villagers, smallholders, freemen and priests mentioned in the doomsday book of 1086 must have come from somewhere, it is probable that they were of Saxon origin from the Saxon settlement of Horbury and they settled not too far away from their relatives on the hill watching over the river.

Having said this it is also a possibility that these settlers to Wakefield were part of the invading Norman army, perhaps they were followers of the military, they would have required priests, cooks and other tradesmen to keep their army marching, or they may have been wards or serfs belonging to the Norman lord who was granted this land.

As for the Vikings, I wish I could say for sure that they had a part in the history of Wakefield, and for so many years, just like most residents of this fair city, I believed it to be of Viking origin and I am as disappointed as I am sure the residents reading this are, but as you have read, the lack of evidence and a few place names unfortunately do not make a Viking settlement.

There are rumors of a Viking burial ground near Gawthorpe, it is known locally as "Fairy Hill", but there is no evidence to support this theory and it is more than likely the location referred to is just a natural mound or deposits from one of the near-by mines which once operated in the area and so without dateable evidence and intrusive exploration of this site we will never know if it is rumor or fact.

When I began writing this book I was very excited to be telling the story of the infamous Romans and Vikings we thought once roamed the land beneath our feet, unfortunately the more I researched the more it became apparent that Wakefield before the Norman invasion of 1066 was not really of much importance in the land, this was soon to change however, with the invasion of our neighbors from across the sea to the south.

6 THE NORMANS

I do realize that up to now, I have not covered the full expanse of years leading up to the Norman Invasion which of course cover what is known as "The Dark Ages"

This is because there is very little information in regards to the 200 or so years, after the Romans departed Britain, and other than the bell pits at Gawthorpe, the abundant forestation, wildlife and the fish populated river which attracted hunters, it wasn't until after William conquered England, that Wakefield became more than merely just a place to hunt, fish and harvest wood.

It would be the invading Norman nobility who brought the small village of Wakefield out of the shade of the great Oaks and set it on its journey of historic importance planting it firmly on the map.

When King William the 1st claimed the throne

of England, he granted generous tracts of land across the length and breadth of the country to his most faithful of knight's who had fought with him at the village of "Battle" near Hastings at the beginning of the invasion in 1066.

In around 1084-86, William the Conqueror granted the Lordship of Wakefield to the first Earl De Warrene, a family name which would begin to shape parts of Wakefield as we know it today along with the Saville's and De Lacy's.

It occurs to me that to continue this volume as a story of Wakefield, would be drifting away from my initial intentions, and as I don't wish to bore people with dates and names in this book (these can be found easily online or in my previous book) I will be moving on from the story of Wakefield and on to theories and questions surrounding events and locations in and around Wakefield.

7 TWO CASTLES

We begin with the questions surrounding Lowe Hill, this earthen mound is known locally as Cannonball Hill and it is a firm favorite location for sledding during the snowy days, and watching concerts at the bandstand which used to stand on top of the hill but was moved to a much larger Tudor looking building at the base of the hill, these concerts are provided free of charge by the local music collective.

Lowe Hill stands proudly, covered by trees in the middle of Clarence Park with commanding views across Wakefield city Centre and much of the surrounding area, it is central to three parks, Thornes park, Clarence Park and Holmfield Park which together make Wakefield Park.

It was originally thought that the nick-name "Cannonball hill" was given to the site after a few cannonballs were discovered there, the rumors spread that these cannonballs were left from the cannons used to fire on, and destroy, Sandal Castle which lies approx. 1.20 miles (2112 Yards) south by south west of Cannonball Hill on the far side of the river.

It is known that "Mons Meg" the great cannon which stands on the battlements of Edinburgh Castle in Scotland, could throw a 19-1/2-Inch iron ball around 1400 yards or a stone ball 2800 yards, so there is a possibility that large cannon similar to Mons Meg were mounted on Lowe Hill, although Mons Meg is of the correct period relating to the destruction of Sandal castle, it is a very large and heavy cannon and so it is doubtful one or more cannon of that size would be dragged up the hill and smaller artillery which was favored by the military of the 17th Century would not reach that distance when shot.

Excavations at the site of Lowe Hill have come up with various theories based on their finds, It was first thought by local historians and early archaeologists that the site was that of an early 12th century wooden fortress, there have been more recent excavations in the last 10 years that dated the site to the 14th Century and describe it as a Motte and Bailey with two possible Bailey's.

One of the theories behind this location is that this site was originally earmarked as the site of a castle to protect the crossing at Chantry Bridge, and it would indeed have been in a good position to protect the river crossing, the site is just over 1000 yards from Chantry bridge, the castle was apparently abandoned before completion, after a terrible storm brought it down and the work was moved to the more advantageous site at Sandal.

This theory does seem very plausible, and I recall reading that there are some records which back up this theory stating that a storm took place in the area around the time, I have not seen the actual records myself and I am struggling to recall where I read the information that records of the storm exist, but there is another theory that I have, which I would like to share.

Perhaps when the Lord De Warrene chose the site of his castle, he informed the mason's that he wanted it building on "the hill" overlooking the River, but did he specify which hill? As already mentioned there are several hills around Wakefield which would have made good strategic locations.

Is it possible that the mason's began their work in the wrong location? Once the mistake had been realized, then the work was abandoned and they moved to the correct site at Sandal?

It could have also been an issue with the land at Lowe Hill; perhaps it was not solid enough for the foundations? This would give us a reason for the two Bailey's, the first being built on unsafe ground and so a second was attempted.

I am not sure what the geological formation of the land beneath Lowe hill is made of although I would have presumed, like much of the ground beneath Wakefield, it would be Sandstone, I do know that the site at Sandal is a natural rocky outcrop making for a much firmer and sturdier foundation, presuming the land at Low Hill isn't rock.

So was the site at Lowe Hill a mistake? Was it a natural obstacle that could not be overcome? Or was it the site of a siege castle? Was the hill natural or was it man-made?

We know that many castles around the country from the Norman invasion were built on natural formations; however there were also many that were built on man-made mounds, although usually siege forts there are examples of more permanent structures being built on a man-made hill.

A brass cannon which was seized from the Russians at the fall of Sevastopol in 1855, stood on the hill in the late 1850's, a cannon that is reported to have been exactly the same stood at Pontefract castle also, so it is more than likely that this was the origin of the Cannonball Hill nick-name.

The location of these cannons, if there were indeed two and it wasn't the same cannon being passed around, is now unknown and they were probably melted down to help the war effort during World War Two, along with the WW1 tank which stood in the park and the cannon which was perched on Sandal Castle for many years (unless this was the same cannon which had possibly been relocated from Lowe Hill).

It is thought that Cromwell's army camped somewhere in the vicinity of Clarence Park before attacking and destroying the castle at Sandal in 1645, two years after the attack on Wakefield in 1643, it is also rumored that Oliver Cromwell himself, spent the night at Low Laithes Farm, a beautiful timber framed building which now houses Low Laithes Golf Club, but again there has been no evidence of this and my attempts to gain permission to metal detect the area of low Laithes for dateable finds were unfortunately denied.

The Normans did more than just establish a castle in the area, a parish church was built on the site of the Anglo-Saxon cross and several Hunting parks were established in the North West and later on the east side of Wakefield.

Hunting lodges were built at Eastmoor, Gawthorpe and Kirkhamgate that we are aware of, there may have been others that were possibly built in villages around Wakefield, these hunting parks belonged to the King and would have contained large amounts of deer and wild boar, and Fortified rabbit warrens will have stood in areas around Wakefield too.

Parts of the hunting lodge at Gawthorpe can still be seen, they are now being used as outbuildings at the top of the hill which stands by the side of a public footpath, running from Gawthorpe Lane to Dogloich Wood.

I have seen a large amount of remnants of broken stone tiles and blocks scattered all over the field that the path runs through and it is quite possible these are from the hunting lodge as very little of the original building remains.

When is a castle not a castle?

One thing that I claimed in my first book was that there may have been more castles in and around the Wakefield area than we know of, including Lowe Hill, Sandal and Horbury castles I can now reveal it does appear that there were others places and buildings, which were referred to as "Castle".

The site of Coney Warren at Lee moor, and the road name Castle Gate Lane which leads up to it, suggests that there may have been a castle in this area, this is further backed up by the name of Castle Head Lane, and Westgate Lane only half a mile or so to the West of Coney Warren.

I have investigated the whole of this area thoroughly, and although the former landowner Mr. Holmes, assured me that he recalled his father and grandfather mentioning a castle on the hill, somewhere in the vicinity of Lee Moor, it appears that the only "castle" in this area is the public house on Leeds road which does indeed stand on a hill.

With this being said, there was a Coney Warren in this area and it is still known as Coney Warren today.

A Coney Warren was a large fortified stone structure with crenellations giving it the appearance of a small castle or fortress where rabbits would have been bred and kept for food.

Perhaps it was the remains of this building that Mr. Holmes Grandfather and Father were discussing? It would be easy to mistake a building such as that as a castle, there are still some examples still standing around the country that we can compare to and many of these were built of a similar design, these do resemble a small castle or fortress.

The road names would have been given to the location long after the Coney Warren was built, and so it appears that there was a castle here, but only in the sense that it was a fortified building, rabbit was only for the rich at the time these buildings were in use and they would have been well protected from poachers.

We are aware that Lindale Hill (Lindle Hill) was once a rabbit warren too, this was said to date back to the Medieval period and so we can safely assume that this too would have been fortified, before I was aware of the laws surrounding metal detecting I did a search on Lindale Hill, I found very few items of interest here, one item was a flat triangular lead object which looked to have come from a trunk or suitcase, there were a few rusty iron bars and a single, very large medieval nail head.

This nail head looks very similar to the type used in church doors and many other medieval dated wooden doors, perhaps this was part of a fortified structure on the hill?

The Templar Connection?

There is information that somewhere around Lofthouse, some land was held by the religious order of the Knights Templar, where this particular plot of land was we do not know, but if this was the case perhaps the castle road names relate to a Preceptory or fortification of this Grand Order of Knights?

We do have to take into account that nor all land held by the Templars was fortified however, it may just have been a simple farmstead or perhaps even a mill that they owned in the area, the information is not very specific.

Which brings me to the site of the "alleged" Roman camp at Lofthouse which is marked on the old maps as a "Roman Marching Camp", Mr. J.W. Walker first excavated this site in the 1930's and he found no evidence of the Romans here, he instead concluded that the shape of the ditched enclosure was "similar" to that of Saxon sites discovered elsewhere in the country.

There were no physical finds from the Saxon period to back up this theory and Mr. Walker was basing this theory on other examples of Saxon farmsteads that had been reported in Britain, as I wrote a full report of this site in my first History of Wakefield book I won't go into too much detail on this one.

I spent several years metal detecting this site and discovered only finds from the 12th Century onwards, other than a single glass bead which was dated to sometime from the Bronze Age through to modern day, all my finds that were of dateable interest hit around the 12th to 15th Century, these included a pocket knife blade, a lead domino and an irregular dice (die).

No religious artefacts or anything relating to the order of the Templar was discovered here, however it is possible that the moated sited was the home of the Knight's, they may have built some kind of fortification even if it was only a defensive ditch and there are no other sites in the area that look to have been fortified.

The Coney Warren at Lee Moor would have been built to provide food for rich people or those of nobility, the Knights Templar were said to live in poverty themselves yet they were a rich and powerful order, they would have required a regular supply of meat even though they would have grown their own vegetables, but would the warren have been so far from the site at Lofthouse? Standing over 1500 yards away, as the crow flies?

It is more than likely that this site at Lofthouse was just a ditched farmstead, the ditch being there to protect the inhabitants and animals from predators which roamed in the nearby woodland forests such as bear and wolves.

Unfortunately the use of Green Waste on this site for the last few centuries has contaminated the site so much that determining if the artefacts found there, were actually dropped there or if they came from the ash works at Leeds, is almost impossible.

Although the site mentioned here, could be a plausible theory as to who owned it, I would suggest that there is another site more suitable for the knights, even though it does not have a moat or ditch surrounding it, this site is very close by to the enclosure.

A modern eco-friendly house now stands among a thick blanket of trees on this plot of land. Once the grand architecture of Lofthouse Hall stood here, it is known that many great halls and houses were built on the foundations of earlier halls and houses or seats of power.

The site of Lofthouse Hall is privately owned and is surrounded by a large wall making visibility onto the land impossible, even using old maps and modern Google Earth images the copse of trees is too thick to penetrate and Lidar has unfortunately not covered this area as yet to allow us a better understanding of the landscape beneath the trees.

The land here is quite vast, and it is of virgin territory in regards to excavation or investigation (to my knowledge), but it does stand on a hill overlooking Lee Moor and slightly to the east of Westgate Lane and Castle-head Lane, are these roads relating to Lofthouse hall or the land it stood on? It does stand at least half a mile west of Castle Gate Lane but it isn't unknown for large buildings to have extensive length driveways or causeways leading to them.

There is also a "Temple View" at Lofthouse, so we have to ask the question, was there a temple in the area? Or is this a reference to the Templar Knight's? I will be doing more research into this area of interest and will publish my finds (if any) in future work.

8 THE BATTLE OF WAKEFIELD, 1460

Moving on to the 15th Century, from the 14th Century, our next query is from the 1400's and covers perhaps Wakefield's most famous claim to historic fame, The Wars of the Roses and the Battle of Wakefield.

I appreciate that I did cover quite an extensive amount of the battle in my previous book, but there were some parts of this important historic event which I felt needed more investigation, and as such I have been able to create some new theories in regards to the battle.

The Battle Of Wakefield in 1460 AD is probably one of the most well-known of tales around Wakefield among its residents, and those with an interest in the Wars of the Roses, many of us grew up clambering amongst the ruins of Sandal castle, sledding down the side of the motte or Bailey into the empty moat or playing in the fields below the shadow of the ruins.

If you were to ask any long-time resident of Wakefield, they would be able to recall at least one memory involving the castle and their lives, it is a special place which commands stunning views and breathes with the ghosts of the past.

There are many written accounts of the events surrounding the battle and the defeat of Richard Duke of York at Manygates, but what is not written is the fate of the Knights whose remains were discovered in 1825, their skeletons were discovered along with swords and spurs by the side of the River Calder below Sandal Castle and very close to where the beck now runs into the river.

Were these attacking Lancastrian force or were they retreating Yorkist knights attempting to escape the carnage unfolding in front of the castle?

We have reliable information taken from archives and historical documentation, that Andrew Trollop and the Earl of Northumberland of the Lancastrian army, had troops waiting close by the river, the battle map I have seen created by other historians however puts Andrew Trollop's troops closest to the spot where the remains were discovered, his troops were waiting for the order to attack, standing close to the banks of the Calder where the beck now runs past Portobello estate and the field below the castle to Kettlethorpe hall lake.

Of course at this time Portobello did not exist and the small beck had not been dug, so this particular area would have been part of the woodland which stretched across where Portobello now stands; Trollops position was around 800 yards from the castle.

During the 15th Century this particular area was marshland to one side and woodland to the other, wet and muddy but an excellent place for knights to await with their horses, hidden among the large trees and bulrushes which would have grown here (and still do along the stream) a great Oak tree stands by one of the bridges crossing the beck which looks as though it is old enough to have seen the action.

This however does not answer the question about the knights remains that were discovered, I have looked at this area on Google Earth, Bing maps and Lidar as well as many historical maps, and I have visited the area on many occasions at varying times of the year, to see if perhaps there had been a crossing in this location, there were no clues given on most of the mapping tools, however the Lidar map does reveal what appears to be a banking below the waterline.

This may be pareidolia, but it is plausible that the river at the time of the battle was shallow enough to wade across.

If the river did run its current course at the time of

the battle then this would add credence to my theory, but it is also a possibility that the river ran a slightly different course and without seeing detailed maps from before the Calder & Hebble Navigation was built it is difficult to say if these Knights were fleeing or cut down where they stood in the woodland.

If they had been discovered more recently this may not have been an issue, we have ways of recording finds such as these now, if these had been available when the remains were first discovered, the information gathered could have told us which way the remains were facing, how they were killed and much more

One of my theories is that the remains discovered in 1825 were those of Yorkist Knights riding away from the castle attempting to escape the battle by crossing the river, here some of them were cut down before they had the chance to cross the water, their steeds dismounting them and galloping away to leave their riders to their fate.

Another theory is that these were Lancastrian Knights under Andrew Trollop's command who were struck down where they stood, before they were able to attack the castle, this however is a little far-fetched as at the time that area was lined with trees and the vast woodland covering where Portobello now stands, any archers shooting from the castle would not have been able to reach the thick woodland with their arrows, let alone penetrate it to the extent of killing someone in armor.

Our next question is why did Richard leave the safety of the walls of Sandal Castle? This was a structure that would have been almost impossible to siege, the food and water supplies would have lasted the occupant's months, although one theory suggests that these were running low.

The main theory that we are taught as to why Richard left the castle is that Richard thought that the Lancastrian forces were much smaller in numbers, he did not know about the troops hiding in the woodland or the marshland where Pugneys now stands and as they approached he boldly attacked thinking he had the upper hand, however he was sorely mistaken and soon over run by the Lancastrian troops who were hidden.

It is also thought that some of his lords may have betrayed Richard, leading him into a trap and defecting to the other side against the Yorkist's, what is known is that Richard was vastly outnumbered and the battle lasted a very short time, some say only 20 minutes of fighting took place and the death toll was predominantly Yorkist.

The site of Richard's death is also questionable, we know that the current monument was placed there during the 19th Century to commemorate the battle and that an earlier monument stood somewhere close by in that area but it was torn down during the

English Civil War.

Some historians believe that Richard got no further than outside the gates of the castle before he was struck down, whereas others say that the fighting reached the park on Manygates Lane and Richard was killed somewhere near there.

The exact spot where he fell will probably never be discovered as it is said that Richard's body was removed, but it is safe to say that with the Yorkist's being outnumbered Richard would have been a target for all Lancastrians, so it is doubtful he got far at all before he met his fate.

I have also heard several theories about the death of the Earl of Rutland but the one thing that most of these do agree on, is that the young Earl reached the site of Chantry Chapel, but from here the stories take different directions.

One of the most well-known stories says that he was helped by a monk who lived in a house by the river crossing, and the Lancastrian soldiers discovered him hiding there cutting him down on the spot, there was a small house at this location for many years although the exact date of it I do not know.

The story that I know most well from school (a long time ago) was that the young Earl ran upstream along the river bank reaching the site where Fall Ings lock now stands before he was captured and killed at this location.

Whatever the truth, we do know that both Richard and the Earl were killed on the 30th December 1460 and we may never know the exact location these two historical men lost their lives perhaps the remains discovered by the river were actually those of Richard and the Earl?

James Roderick O'Flanagan (1814-1900) was a writer and historian and he gives a "detailed" account of the young Earl's fate. However just like J.W Walker and other authors of their time there are inaccuracies.

O'Flanagan gives the date of the battle as Christmas Eve, December 24th 1460, where as many others give the date of the battle as the 30th December 1460, as I mentioned above.

O'Flanagan then states that the Earl was urged by his tutor, a priest by the name of Robert Aspell, to flee for his life, in many accounts of this act it is said that the Earl of Rutland was struck down in a revenge attack by Lord Clifford as justice for the death of his father in a previous battle.

O'Flanagan's account of the Earls fate states that it was his tutor who pleaded for the young man's life and does not give a location but it appears that many historical writings about this particular event place it on or close to Chantry Bridge, it is plausible that the area from where the "Ruddy Duck" public house now stands which is known as Fall Ings to the point known as Fall Ings Lock may actually refer to the bend in the river where the new Hepworth Gallery stands.

If this is correct then it places the Earl of Rutland's death site as somewhere between the Calder and Hebble Navigation cut at the junction of Barnsley road and Doncaster Road to the Chantry Bridge and anywhere in between perhaps beneath where the old mills which stand close to Barnsley Road and behind the Hepworth Gallery, or beneath the flats off Doncaster Road close to Chantry bridge.

9 AN UNKNOWN CASTLE & AN UNKNOWN BATTLE.

We now move on from the battle of Wakefield to a possible unrecorded or unknown battle which is said to have taken place near Wakefield at the village of Newlands which stand between Wakefield and Altofts, this is a particular place of interest to many of Wakefield's residents, it is also shrouded in mystery as much as it is history.

Before we get into this "unknown" battle though, I would like to introduce you to the history of Newlands.

Newlands is an abandoned village which stands on the river Calder close to Altofts and although strictly not in Wakefield it is part of the Wakefield and five towns and our history and is a site of special interest to myself and many other historians.

I shall begin by explaining what a Preceptory was.

A Preceptory was a place of special value run by either the Knights Templar or the Knights of St John (Hospitallers) it was a farm where crops would be grown and animals farmed, as much as it was a fortress and a "bank", where Pilgrims would deposit their worldly goods of cash and jewelry in return for a Chit which they could then cash in on their arrival in the Holy Land.

One of the earliest known Preceptors of Newlands was one of the Knights Hospitallers called Simon Pacable in 1313 the records predating this are sketchy in detail

There was a dock on the riverside where goods were transported to and from the Preceptory, and as far as I am aware this has now vanished with nothing remaining to show the exact location it stood, although as you will read further in this piece the Preceptory may not have been in the village and the river course may have been much further inland than it is now.

On the modern Google Earth image we can see the remnants of a tributary or stream which runs approx. 300 yards to the north east of where the river now runs and on the north side of the village, it appears as though this was much wider at one time as parts are quite wide in places and if this was the original river course, it would place the dock in what is now a field, just north west of the gun club which was there until recently.

The title deeds for Newlands, which were held by late local historian Mr. John Goodchild until 2006, date back to the 12th and 13th Centuries. These deeds show the generous tracts of land held by this, once powerful, military order of the knights of St

John.

Included in these deeds are several properties and farms at Newlands, including Newlands hall, the Coach house (which still stands) and several outbuildings many of which have now crumbled leaving only dilapidated shell filled with rubble and overgrown with brambles, nettles and ivy.

According to some historians, the village of Newlands was established in the year 1213 by King John of England as a Preceptory apparently for the Knights Templar until the year 1256 when the lands were handed over to the Templars rivals the Knights Hospitallers or Knights of St John.

Why this transposition took place we cannot say, most of the Templar lands were not handed to the Hospitallers until 1312 when Edward II declared the Templar order outlaws and granted the Hospitallers all the Templars goods and land, as mentioned earlier it is said that the Templar order had land at Lofthouse however more research is required into this.

If indeed Newlands was a Preceptory of the Templars then this would make it one of only Preceptory's in Yorkshire, it has been established that Yorkshire was the largest stronghold for the Knights Templar in the Country so we cannot rule out the possibility that they held a Preceptory here.

Personally I think it is doubtful that the Templar

held this land at all and more likely that it was given directly to the Knights of St John and owned by the Crown previous to this as it does not make any sense why land owned by the Templar would be given to a rival order in a time when the Templar were in favor.

Early in its history the Preceptory was the beneficiary of a powerful patron, Roger Le Peytvin Lord of the manor of Altofts and later William Lyvett of Altofts hall in 1447. The property was dissolved by Henry the VIII who then bestowed the property upon himself.

Now we have covered the brief history behind the origin of Newlands, I discovered a poem written in the late 18th Century and credited to Mr. Benjamin Clarkson which recounts the dissolution of the Knights of Newlands.

This Ballad written in four parts gives a very detailed account of a proposed battle which took place between the Yeoman of Wakefield and the Knights of Newlands.

The following is taken from the book: The Battle of Newlands a poem in four parts, the writing of which has not been dissected before to determine if it is a work of fiction or if it is based on true events.
The beginning of the book starts with a letter alerting a publisher to the poem, the author of the letter is not the author of the poem.

The author of the poem begins with the following:

Several well-known circumstances which happened some years ago in the town and neighborhood of Wakefield, gave rise to the following Ballad: The writer has only to observe, that as it was not composed with intent to give offence to any one, he hopes it will perused with good-nature.

It is not clear what the author means here, is he admitting that the poem is to be taken light heartedly? And not as a serious account of the "circumstances" of just that he meant no offence with his account of the battle?

THE ARGUMENT.

King Harry sends the Wakefield men
To fight their Newland Foes:
Sir Richard Rich doth lead them on,
But talks before he goes:
Encouraged by the maidens fair
They march in proud array,
(Their kinsfolks leaving safe at home)
To Newland wend their way.

The Battle of Newland
Part The First
When good king Henry* riled this land
He ruled with sov'reigh sway;
The like before were never seen,
Nor since unto this day.

There lived at Newland ** castle strong,
Of Knights*** full many a score,
Who would not legiance pay the King,
Nor do him service more.

Nor was that all, for they did send
Defiance to the King,
To fight as many men as he
Into the field would bring.

*King Henry VIII A.D. 1540
**Near Wakefield, Yorkshire.
*** Knights Templars, commonly called Knights of St John of Jerusalem.

To check their stubborn high-blown pride
And make them quiet yield,
The King this letter wrote unto
The Mayor of Wakefield*.

"I charge you on your legiance due,
"As you shall answer me,
"Ye arm the yeomen of your town
"Without delay or fee.

"And straitway unto Newland go,
"Subdue that slavish crew
"And in what manner this is done
"ye unto me shall shew."

The May'r forthwith together called
The townsfolks in a trice,
To know what best were to be done
In the affair so nice.

Then stept there forth a gallant Knight,
Sir Richard Rich** by name;
A nobler Knight did ne'er appear
In quest of early fame.

*Formerly a borough town.
**Then the Chancellor of the court of Augmentations, afterwards created Lord Rich

His father's only son was he,
Of birth and lineage high
And he with youthful ardour burnt
His skill in fight to try.

With modest, yet with manly grace
Which every heart did own,
He bowed, thus bespoke the May'r
And Yeoman of the town.

"Shall Rage and Discord rule the land,
"Shall War and Famine thrive
"While Peace and Plenty banished far,
"We scarce be left alive.

"Let not our hearts of courage fail,
"but now be firm and true;
"Let us march forth with bowmen bold
"The castle to subdue.

"Then shall our great heroic fame
"spread round through all the land,
"When gallantly we shall have fought
"At Henry our King's command:

"Besides we shall have large rewards
"In ready gold and fee;
"In English gold it will be told,
"Both men and yeomanry."

He said- and shouts of joy were heard
Through all the town to ring;
"Long live Sir Richard Rich," they cried,
"Sir Richard and the King;
"There's not a Knight in Wakefield town,
"Nor yet in all the land,
"So gallant as Sir Richard is,
"And he shall us command."

The forth appeared threescore yeomen

Young yeomen spruce and gay.
The down appeared upon their chin,
And blithe as larks were they.

In sword and cross-bow fight well skilled,
And eke in bow and arrows;
Nor were there in the north country
So famed for shooting sparrows.

With drawer and singlets lilly white,
Their doublets cheerful green,
With scarlet faced and silver laced,
Round hats with plumes therin.

Their bows of toughest yew were made,
Their arrows sharp and long,
And on their proud and manly thigh
A stout broad sword there hung.

Their quivers o'er their shoulders thrown
Were buckled fast before,
Their bows then slackened and unstrung
In their left hand they bore.

With flags and streamers azure blue,
Beset with lillies* gay,
And drums and trumpets, flutes and horns,
They stood in proud array.

While this prepared and resolved
To conquer or to die,
Coming to lead them to the fight
Their Captain they did spy.

*The town arms of Wakefield

Sir Richard on a coal-black steed
With golden trappings gay,
In arms and armour bright he shone
The rival of the day.

The prancing steed well trained for war,
Nor frightened with the sword,
He champt, he foamed, and proudly neighed
Beneath his noble lord.

With shouts the heroes greet their chief,
The drums and trumpets sound;
They march : their nimble willing feet
Beat time upon the ground.

Most sure it was a gallant site
As ever Wakefield saw,
The noble Captain and his men
All marching in a row.

And as they marched through merry Wakefield
So blithesome and so gay,
The maidens all with one accord
Most lovingly did say:

"Be stout and bold, ye merry men,
"Fight as you hold us dear;
"And if you conquer your proud foe,
"Our love ye need not fear."

And now they march in proud array
And leave the town behind,
Gallant and gay their sable plumes
Now wantoned in the wind.

And as they marched through woods and meads
Twas wondrous to see
The frighted kine, the bucks and does
All bounding o'er the lee.

When they in sight of Newland came,
To all men be it told,
The heroes one and all did look
More cheerful and more bold.

*As when the scenting hounds have found
The covert of a hare,
With savage joy the promised game
For chace they do prepare.*

*So did the heroes stout and bold,
Joyful their bows they strung,
The noble feats of Chevy Chace
They all in concert sung.*

*Here ends the first part of my song.
The battle's yet to come,
And he that dare not go to fight
E'en let him stay at home.*

THE END OF THE FIRST PART.

In this first part of the poem the author describes Newlands as a castle, he also suggests that the knights were in large numbers "many a score strong", as the author describes the order given to attack Newlands he gives us an insight as to why it was ordered, King Henry is of course Henry VIII, he was responsible for the dissolution of the monasteries which would have included the religious order of the knights of St John.

THE ARGUMENT

*The castle of the Newland Knights,
Their arms and horses too
Are sung-and they like trusty Knights
Stand to their leader true.
Sir Claret Vine doth lead them on:
The battle does begin;
Both Knights and Heroes, well I wis,*

Do slash through thick and thin.

THE BATTLE OF NEWLAND
PART THE SECOND

Within a spacious lowly vale
Part bounded by a wood,
And other part by Calder* washed,
There Newland Castle stood.

The castle it was built most strong
With gilded turrets crown'd
So fair it seemed a palace built
Upon enchanted ground.

The Holy Knights who dwelt therat,
For feats of chivalry
They one and all most famous were
Throughout the whole country.
*River Calder

The chief and captain of the train,
Sir Claret Vine by name,
Sir Vinyard Port the second was,
From holy land they came.

The rest from different kingdoms were
Assembled there together,
As ships into the harbour sail
To moor in stormy weather.

In armour clad from head to foot
The Knights they did appear,
And pendant from their shining breasts
A silver cross did wear.

Their right hand grasped a trembling spear,
Their left arm bore a shield,
And on their thigh a flaming sword,
They knew full well to wield.

Each mounted on a milk white steed
In silent order waits
The marching of their warlike foe,
Within the castle gates.

So silent wait the wary cats
To catch unwary food;
Nor with more dreadful silence wait
The tigers of the wood.

When Lo' upon the neighb'ring hills
Come winding thro' the wood,
The warlike folk Sir Vinyard spied,
As on the wall he stood.

Then thus unto the Knights he spake:-
"We have not much to fear,
"A Captain and but threescore men
"Do in the field appear.

"So resolute and bold a foe
"I never yet did see,
"Nor in such jocund merry mood
"As all his men and he.

"But sure they soon will graver be
"If I divine aright,
"If they with us dare to engage
"And mix in dreadful fight."

The Wakefield heroes stout and bold
Now to the castle come,
Right glad were they and eke well pleased
To find the Knights at home.

Sir Richard Rich first drew his sword
And then rode on before,
Nor stopt until he nigh had come
Unto the castle door.

Then raising on his stirrup high
He thus aloud did say:-
"In the King's name I charge you all
"That ye do me obey.

"Your castle now to me give up,
"Your goods and chattels all,
"Your arms lay down, so shall ye 'scape
"This once a dreadful thrall.

"But if your proud and haughty hearts
"Refuse the just demands,
"Without delay ye all shall feel
"The strength of our right hands

Sir Claret mounted on his steed
And brandishing his lance,
In 'fiance of the challenge sent
Forth forward did advance.

"Ye simple, silly, senseless race,
"Ye beardless boys," he said,
"Think you to fright us with your looks
"As you would fright a maid?

"Go get you back from whence you came,
"And keep your doors within;
"Take my advice 'tis best to sleep
"Without a broken skin.

"Yet if your little mock-fight souls
"Dare us in battle meet
"We will not take you thus at odds
"But fairly on our feet."

He said: they one and all alight
From off their warlike steeds;
Each steed returned unto his stall,
And there in quiet feeds.

Now either foe prepared stand
The battle to begin,
Firmly resolved all to die,
Or else the day to win.

Grant me, great God of War, to sing,
Or tell me how to say,
Who in battle fought most stout
And who did run away.

Sir Claret Vine threw up his spear
As signal for the war,
And shouts from all the warriors sent
Were heard both near and far.

The Knights first on St. John did call
To aid them in the fight;
St George, aloud the heroes cried
Defend our King his right.

The Wakefield archers stout and bold
Their fury none could stay;
Full thick they did their arrows send,
Which kept the Knights at bay.

By the third flight of arrows sent
The Knights were galled so
That ten were wounded, and nine sent
Down to the shades below.

The Newland Knights their jav'lins shook,
But with bad aim they threw
Hissing they cut the liquid air,
But never a hero slew.

Like light'ning quick the arrows flew,
The jav'lins thick were sent;
With these the Knights were galled sore,
While these in the air were spent.

With grief Sir Claret Vine he saw
His men so fast to drop;
He called Sir Vinyard to his aid
The furious foe to stop.

Their swords they from their scabbards drew
And thus aloud did cry,
"Ye Knights now let your fury burn,
"And let the wretches die."

They said; The Knights with drawn broad sword
To fight the Heroes flew;
The Heroes cast aside their bows,
Their shining blades they drew.

Now Knights and Heroes all are mixed
Primiscuous in the field,
All fight, some fly, and some pursure,
But all refuse to yield.

In all a sense of honour rise,
And every warrior warms
Amidst the danger, dreadful din,
And all the clash of arms.

So little wanton boys engage
Whole squadrons of armed wasps;
Each warrior bent on deeds of fame,
He runs, he fights, and grasps.

They closed and fought four hours long,
Nor yet could either say
(In fight they were so equal matched)
Which side would win the day.

Thus hand to hand in dreadful fight
Were mixed the warlike throng:-
Which bring be about half way through
This most heroic song.

THE END OF THE SECOND PART.

In the first two sentences of the Second Part of this poem, the author describes the location of the castle.

Part bounded by a wood, And other part by Calder washed, There Newland Castle stood.

The castle it was built most strong, With gilded turrets crown'd. So fair it seemed a palace built, Upon enchanted ground.

There is some woodland remaining in the area, although it is doubtful that many of the trees which grow there now, actually belonged to the woodland mentioned there is one very large thick tree which looks to be at least 500 years old standing close to the river, although without dendrochronology investigation it is difficult to date this tree and I am only estimating the age based on the enormity of the tree.

The banks of the River Calder are very close to both the village and the location I believe the suggested castle may have actually stood.

This part of the ballad mentions three main characters (not including the King and Queen). The first is Sir Richard Rich who we know was Thomas Cromwell's right hand man, we are also aware that Thomas Cromwell was directly involved with the dissolution of the monasteries, he was a factual historical figure, but then we come across Sir Claret

Vine and Sir Vinyard Port.

These latter two names were referred to as Knights of St John, however having contacted the museum of the Knights of St John I was informed that there was no record of any Knights of that name in their archives from that period.

With this information it makes me wonder if these names were created from "artistic license", were they a creation of the author perhaps? If so, how much of the Ballad, if any, is actual truth? And how much is the fantasy of an over active imagination.

Perhaps these names were used as a nod to the wine brewing that we know monks and religious men were famed for, Claret Vine for example being red wine, the name Vinyard Port appears to be somewhat more obvious, a vineyard being a place where grapes are grown and port a type of wine.

THE BATTLE OF NEWLAND

PART THE THIRD.

THE ARGUMENT.
The merry battle sill is sung,
And many a feat is played,
No gallant hero bold doth wish
At home that he had staid.
At length the Knights they vanquish'd are,
Their castle eke is taken;
Some Wakefield Heroes bold are slain,
And some do save their bacon.

Sir Richard Rich, right glad to see

The Knights so fast to fall,
To chear his valiant warlike men
He thus aloud did call:

"Fight on, fight on , my merry blades
"Fight on as ye bagan;
"So from our shinging bright broad swords
"Shall 'scape us ne'er a man."

The Newland Knights full vexed were,
And eke they grieved sore,
For never were they in a fight
So closely pressed before.

Sir Vinyard 'spied young Bertram out,
(A Wakefield Hero gay,
Who with his own right trusty sword
Three sturdy Knights did slay,)

The Knight he on the Hero fell,
An hour they fought full sore,
The Knight the Hero's heart blood drew,
Who word spake never more.

The Wakefield Heroes grieved sore
To see young Bertram fall,
For sure he fought this bloody day
The valiant'st of them all.

Sir Claret Vine attacked was
By three Heroes together
To brave the storm or quiet yield
The Knight he knew not whether.

The Heroes stuck so wonderous close
He could not get away,
So like a baited bull he stood
And kept the foes at bay.

At length the Knight with his broad sword

One Hero he struck down:
Another, sickened at the sight,
Fell in a deadly swoon.

The third and stoutest of them all
Fought on with might and main;
He struck the Knight upon his crest,
Which made him mad with pain.

The Knight he aimed a deadly stroke,
The Hero aimed one too,
Their clashing swords then met betwixt
And into shivers flew.

The Wakefield Hero, tired with
The labours of the day,
His back to the proud foe he turned
And numbly tripped away.

Sir Claret Vine he with full speed
The Hero followed hard,
And thrice the flying foe pursued
All round the castle yard.

At length run down and wearied out
They came unto a tree;
The Hero claspt his arms around,
" A boon, a boon," quoth he.

"No boon I'll grant thee, but thou shalt
"Into the river go,"
Replied the Knight, and griped hard
By th' neck and heels the foe.

He whirled the Hero in the air
Full twelve yards high and more,
So high the like were never done
By mortal man before.

As round do turn the windmill sails

When by the tempest tost,
So turned the hero and so fast
All vital sense he lost.
Or like the fragment of a rock
By some huge giant thrown
Into the air, so up he rose,
And so he tumbled down.

And as he passed all through the air
So lightsome and so gay,
Sir Claret Vine unto the foe
Most spitefully did say:

"Thou fliest lightly, by my troth,
"Excuse my vulgar whim;
"So chuse thee, chuse thee, good fellow
"Whether thou'lt sink or swim,"

In Calder's limpid stream he fell,
Far from the brink so gay,
The finny fry were all amazed,
And scudded fast away.

Lord what a splash the Hero made!
How did the waters fly!
Not more when Jove amongst the frogs
Their King sent from the sky.

The Wakefield Heroes saw him fall,
In haste they dragged him ou;
Though sadly drenched and sore afraid
He soon grew strong and stout.

Meantime both Knights and Heroes fought,
They did so kick and cuff,
Their arms they laid about as if
They ne'er would have eough.

Thus they stormed, and fought and raged
Four hours more that day;

Who would the battle win or lose
No one not yet could say.

At length three Heroes fierce and bold
A solemn vow did make,
To lose their lives or else in fight
Sir Vinyard Port to take.

Then forth they rushed into the midst,
Where they Sir Vinyard found,
And with a deep and deadly stroke
They felled him to the ground.

As falls the stately mountain oak,
The forest's pride and King,
So fell the Knight, and with the fall
His polished arms did ring.

And frantic with his dying pain
The Knight was heard to call,
"Revenge my death upon the foe,
"Or curse light on you all."

Sir Claret Vine, who in the fight
Had been so sore opprest,
They with a fell and fatal stab
Sent the proud Knight to rest.

The Wakefield Heroes gave a shout
Which did the Knights appall,
Their courage drooped when they saw
Their noble Captains fall.

The Heroes then upon the Knights
So close their swords were lain,
That many a valiant holy Knight
Lay gasping on the plain.

The Knights now found the Heroes would
No quarter give nor day;

"Alack!" they cried, "Not one must 'scape,
"Good lack and well o' day!"

Full sorely galled on every side
The Knights were forced to yield,
The Wakefield Heroes did remain
Sole masters of the field.

With shouts the Heroes rent the skies,
Their joy as great it were
As when the hunters have pursued
And killed the trembling deer.

God lack, it was a piteous sight
To look upon the slain!
To see so many valiant Knights
Extended on the plain!

Of six score Knights who marched out
To brave the foe to fight,
But twenty 'scaped, the rest were sent
Down to the shades of night.

Of threescore Wakefield Heroes bold,
Who fought this bloody day,
Twice ten were wounded, five were killed,
And five did run away.

Twas on the day of Lammas-tide
This bloody fight was won,
Nor did they end the sad day's work
But with the setting sun.

The castle doors now opened wide
And a free entrance gives.
In marched the Heroes and the place
Strait a new Lord receives.

A bloodier battle ne'er was fought

Historical Mysteries Of Wakefield

Than this, by mortal men,
Nor e'er a bloodier fight than this
Will Newland see again.

THE END OF THE THIRD PART.

Here the author describes in great detail the battle which ensued between the "Wakefield Yeoman" and the knights of Newlands.

This part of the ballad also gives us both a time period and approximate year of the battle.

The ballad tells us that the battle was fought on Lammas-tide, also known as Lammas day, this is a holiday celebrated in some English speaking countries in the Northern Hemisphere, usually between 1st August and 1st September to mark the annual wheat harvest.

As such we now know that the battle took place sometime in the month of August or the first day of September in either 1540 or 1541, and although Mr. Clarkson refers to the Knight's Templar being dissolved in 1540 we know that this is incorrect as the Knight's Templar were dissolved in England in 1312, four years after King Philip of France declared war on the order of Templar's.

In the fourth part of the ballad we are informed that Catherine is the name of Henry VIII's wife at the time of the battle:

Right glad to hear it was the King

*As he sat in his chair,
And rising slow from off his seat
With Catherine so fair*.*

The asterix depicts a footnote which reads: *Lady Catherine Howard, Niece to the Duke of Norfolk queen 1540-1541*

THE ARGUMENT

*The Knights who were in battle slain
The Heroes do entomb,
With well-earned laurels all must grant
The Heroes do go home.
The Wakefield folks well please are
To end the bloody strife;
King Harry says he never knew
The like in all his life.*

*THE BATTLE OF NEWLAND
PART THE FOURTH.*

*Sir Richard bade his men to seek
Young Bertram out with care;
To inter the youth with honours due
The Heroes next prepare.*

*The body borne upon a bier:
A sable pall thrown o'er,
On that the bow and bright broad sword
Which he in battle bore.*

*Twice six young Heroes marched before,
Their arms reversed were,
Twice three support the sable pall
The rest marched in the rear.*

While drums and trumpets, flutes and horns
N mournful accents sound,
Silent and sad, with solemn pace
They bore him to the ground.

"Now fare thee well!" the Captain said,
"Thy fame shall spread around,
"Whilst thy remains, O gallant youth,
"Lie mouldring in the ground."

A more accomplished gentleman
Did Wakefield never see;
A scholar, soldier, duteous son
And sincere friend was he.

Near to a solemn lonely grove
Of beech and polar shade,
The Heroes made on common grave,
And there the Knights were laid.

An obelisk of marble stone
Upraied theron they place,
Awfully grand full long it stood
With ornamental grace.

In well-wrought characters of gold,
Which glittered in the sun,
The warriors next inscribed thus
The monumental stone.

"Stay passenger, whoe'er thou art,
"And look upon this stone;
"If on good errand thou art bound
"Stay not-go-quick pass on.

"But if on lawless errand bent,
"O stop, thyself to save!
"Least thou, like us, too soon do meet
"With an untimely grave."

The news had now reach to the town
How all the Knights were slain,
And that the Wakefield Warriors were
Returning home again.

The townsfolk all with one accord
To meet them did prepare;
Without the town they happy met,
With shouts they rent the air.

They place Sir Richard in a car
Bedecked with gold around,
And with a wreath of laurel green
They next the Hero crown'd.

Nor did the damsels of the town
Neglect their favourite dears;
A true blue knot with laurels set
Each favoured warrior wears.

The banners broad and streamers gay
First in the throng appear,
The Warriors next in order march,
Their bright drawn swords they bear.

The milk white coursers of the Knights
With flowing manes most fair,
(Next to the noble deeds of arms
Their masters chiefest care)

Were led by pages fair and fine,
And they as trophies bore
The battered helms, shields, spears and swords
The vanquish'd Knights had wore.

Preceded by a warlike band
Of music sounding loud,
The Hero next drawn in the car

Was seen above the croud.

Drawn by twelve strong and stout yeomen
Who laurel wreaths did wear,
And next the yeomen of the town
On horseback closed the read.

With shouts they marched all round the town,
The merry bells did ring,
The people never were more glad
At crowning of a King.

It was resolved by them all
To send to London town
To claim the honours of the fight
And make the wonders known.

Two messengers did strait set off
All in a chariot rare,
With streamers flying at the top
Like wild beasts to a fair.

The messengers unto the King
At Court they did repair,
Where they before the King were brought
And Catherine* so fair.

They told the tidings of the fight,
How all the Knights were kill'd,
The castle taken, and that by
The Heroes of Wakefield.

Right glad to hear it was the King
As he sat in his chair,
And rising slow from off his seat
With Catherine so fair*.

Unto the welcome messengers
Who did the tidings bring
Most courteous and most graciously

Thus spoke the joyful King:

"Our thanks we send unto your town
"Your men and yeomanry;
"We have not now within our realm
"Such valiant men as ye.

*Lady Catherine Howard, Niece to the Duke of Norfolk 1540-1541Queen to Henry VIII. Whom he married in the year 1540, in which year the order of Knights Templars was abolished by act of parliament.

"So great a victory ne'er were gained
"Oe'er foes as this by ye;
"For ever of this galliant deed
"Whitness shall Newland be.

"Were but our English subjects all
"So valiant and so true,
"We need not fear what France or Spain
"Or all our foes could do.

"The goods and chattels of the Knights,
"Their corn, their wine and oil,
"We freely give you for reward
"So fair divide the spoil."

God save our Country and our King,
And grant that wars may cease,
That we and all good quiet folks
May end our days in peace

THE END OF THE BALLAD

The final part of the ballad gives us the story of the

aftermath, it tells us that those who died at the battle were brought into Wakefield, here they were buried in a grove of Beech trees and a large obelisk was erected to mark the mass grave, I will be discussing this monument further on in this book.

We know that the Knights of St John were dissolved in 1540 and the Knights Templar and their involvement with Newlands, seem to be a common misconception and perhaps a misinterpretation of the documents and manuscripts which survive in regards to Newlands.

The ballad also refers to Newlands as a "Castle" throughout the whole verse, and with this in mind I began to look around at the land which is close to the village, this location is not within the protected heritage ground and after some time I discovered an area that appears to have an oval shaped banking, this stands on the northern side of the village, two fields over.

Closer examination of this location on Google Earth revealed what appear to be crop marks, these look like they could be the remains of a long causeway with one or two buildings on either side, the causeway heads in the direction of the village, ending at a large square shaped building seated within the oval banking, could this be the Castle of Newlands? And if so did the battle actually take place?

We know that Mr. Clarkson (if indeed it was him

who wrote the poem, as there is speculation that he may not have been the author) was a well-respected historian and author, but where did he acquire his information from to give such a detailed account of the battle?

During the 19th Century there were vineyards quite close to Newlands, these were situated near Heath Hall (not Heath old hall) but how long these had been in operation I cannot say, perhaps if they were growing grapes for wine in the 1800's who is to say that these vineyards were not in operation during the 16th Century too.

After the dissolution of the monasteries by Henry VIII the land at Newlands was sold on to the Bunny family of Newton in 1544, and then in the 1700's it passed hands once more to the Silvester's. It was this family who built Newland Hall, quite possibly adapting and destroying much of the Preceptory buildings in the process including the chapel.

Perhaps the castle still exists in the remnants of the 18th century buildings which stand in ruins on the estate, much of the stonework within these remains is elegantly carved, and there is also the remains of a coat of arms embedded above the doorway of one of the larger buildings, this has been worn down so much by the elements that only the shape of a shield can be seen and nothing remains of the coat of arms that once adorned its surface.

The hall at Newlands was demolished in 1917 but

the village was occupied right up to the 1970's, it was around this time the decline of Newlands began and the remaining families were forced to move, this was due to subsidence caused by the St John's and Park Hill collieries tunnels which ran beneath the village.

The buildings which remain in ruins on the site mainly date from the 1700's and include a couple of 20th Century buildings, it appears to me that if there was a castle at this location then the stone was taken to build the estate of Newlands.

The land eventually became the ownership of the Warmfield brickworks company in 1926 and is now in the hands of a local farmer.

A population Census recorded 78 inhabitants of the village in 1861, this dropped down to only 41 in 1931 and 9 in 1971, when the last family moved out. Since 1971 there have been no residents at the village other than squatters, children and the odd hunter searching for pigeon or rabbit.

Strengthening work was carried out on the early buildings by St John's colliery and they used locally made St John's bricks from the nearby brickworks (the chimney of this can still be seen by the track leading to the estate). Later buildings were repaired and built using bricks from the Normanton Brick Company.

There have been many tales told by locals of their

experiences at Newlands, the village is now in a desperate state of ruin and much of it is overgrown, there are deep cellars which are hidden amongst the undergrowth of bracken, brambles and ivy, a veritable pitfall of traps for any unwary explorer who ventures off the public footpaths which run through the village.

Many reports and stories of a "large beast" have been told, there are some of these stories on the Facebook group "Spooky Goings on in Yorkshire". Some people say that it is a large cat like creature which wanders among the trees, others swear that they saw a wolf or large dog which watches from a distance and never approaches, and there has even been reports of an "ape" like creature which stood its ground against a car before disappearing into the night, the village is so overgrown with trees and scrub that any animal could be living there and no one would know.

A few years ago I was lucky enough to speak with a lady who once found a gold ring at the site with the inscription "for my love" in French on the band, I believe she said that the museum had dated it to the 1500's so this could quite possibly have belonged to one of the knights who were killed, perhaps it belonged to one of the later lords of the manor (or their wife/lover) or even one of the Yeoman of Wakefield, if indeed the battle was factual.

The fact that the inscription was in French is not unusual, however it is known that many of the

Knights were foreigners, and of course there would have been Frenchmen amongst the ranks of the Knights Hospitallers.

What is known is that there is an unprecedented air of mystery surrounding the location, the history can be felt amongst the trees and rubble filled ruins, and as you wander along the public footpaths running between the ruins and woodland, you are almost transported back in time to when this was a bustling village filled with laughter and merriment.

Newlands and the land it is on is of national historic importance and as such is protected by the crown and English Heritage, if we add the above information to the fact that it is also built close to the edge of an ancient barrow at Birkwood (less than half a mile away) and apparently close to the defensive ditch which once surrounded Normanton, although I am unsure of this latter "fact" as Newlands is quite a distance from Normanton as we know it today, but it is very clear to see the great importance of this forgotten village.

An archaeological survey and dig took place in the 1970s on the South side of the village but no evidence of the Preceptory was found, there are still remnants of the wall which surrounded the estate and the majority of this surrounds the North side, it is now crumbling and in need of repair, like much of Newlands the wall has been attacked by ivy and tree branches and it is quite surprising how any of the structures here remain upright.

So did a battle take place and was there a castle at Newlands? I cannot say definitively that the ballad is based on "fact" the only evidence we have that there MAY have been a castle is the suggested earthworks and crop marks I have discovered on Google Earth, I have it on good authority that the new HS2 high speed train route is to run directly through this precise site, as such I have not pursued investigating it further because archaeological excavations are taking place all along the route of the HS2 and this location will be investigated thoroughly in the coming months/years.

I hope that I am correct in my deciphering of the ballad and that the Author has based it on facts, but as we are aware, sometimes theories can be incorrect and I am fully prepared to be proved wrong if it is the case, yet to think that there may be a previously unknown battle and a castle that were not recorded is quite exciting and I look forward to seeing what is discovered there.

10 TUNNELS

The tunnels which run beneath Wakefield have been one of the main subjects that poke its head out on social media on a regular basis, I did cover some information regarding these in my first book, and at the risk of repeating myself I would like to give some kind of concluding answer to my readers regarding this subject.

We shall begin with the "tunnels" discovered beneath the Old Vicarage, we know that there was a building on this site dating back to at least 1584, possibly earlier, and if we look at other large buildings of this period it is easy to imagine the size of this house.

The Rectory House was a three-gabled house, a large building made of a solid oak framework and filled in with masonry of brick and stone facings; the doorways, mullions of the windows, external string-courses, and fireplaces were made of wrought stone, the whole structure being a plain, yet substantial and picturesque building.

The mullioned windows contained diamond-leaded lights, and on one of the ceilings was inscribed the date 1584, evidently, from the architectural appearance of the house, the date of its re-building, so this is evidence that there was a building on this site before the date above.

Many halls and large houses dating to the 16th Century of a similar build were very well constructed with solid foundations stretching the length and width of the building (sometimes further beneath the ground) with connecting cellars for storage of food or wine.

I spoke to the gentleman from Modern Savage Tattoo Studio who was lucky enough to enter the tunnels in 2005 after his friend's dog entered them through a hole in the car park tarmac, he stated that after descending through the tarmac he emerged inside what appeared to be an old brick walled cellar with exits running in several directions.

It is my belief that the "tunnels in this area" are nothing more than cellars from the original building which stood on the site, I believe that Mr. John Goodchild did explore these tunnels at one time, following them for around 100 feet toward the Cathedral and I believe he also confirmed that these were indeed cellars dating to the 16th Century.

The footprint of the house did not run in the direction of the buildings which now stand on

Zetland Street, these new buildings run east to west, the three gabled house which predated these stood north to south and would have crossed Zetland Street, had it been there at the time. This would explain why the gentleman from Modern Savage emerged in the cellars of the Masons lodge which stands opposite the old vicarage.

This may be disappointing to some, but as with much of the information gathered for this book I aim to tell the truth as we know it, as such we have to ask the question; what is the definition of a tunnel?

The Oxford definition is an artificial underground passage, especially one built through a hill or under a building, road, or river.

So we can still refer to these adjoining cellars as "tunnels" as there would have been passage between them, even though these cellars do not represent how we associate something with the word tunnel to appear, if we are to suggest the word tunnel to any person, it conjures up images of roughly carved stone or rock and not brick lined passages, despite the fact these too can be called tunnels.

The alleged tunnel from the Raven to the Cathedral is something that is reminiscent of other religious sites, many of which had short tunnels leading out of the building used by the clergy/monks during the dissolution of the monasteries as escape routes.

These tunnels were also used by local gentry, people who did not wish to have to pass the poor and destitute who would wait around outside the Cathedral for Alms, there is nothing really sinister about this particular tunnel that we are aware of and the reason for it being blocked up may never be revealed, I do believe that this tunnel exists and as I recall I mentioned in my previous book that there was an area in the crypt of the cathedral that I remember visiting as a young child, this has now been blocked off but it is my belief that the tunnel entrance/exit was in this room along with the marble effigy of a knight.

I was a young child at the time (around 7-8yrs old I think) and so I have to allow for some discrepancies in my memory and as the doorway to this chamber is now blocked we will never know if my memory is serving me correctly, unless there are others in the area who also remember this.

As for the other alleged tunnels around Wakefield such as the Court house, Chantry Chapel and the Police station, there is no proof these exist, however recently (in 2016) the landlord of a public house on King Street discovered a loose brick in his venue.

Upon removal of the brick, he says that he could see arched vaulted ceilings and a long tunnel heading in the direction of Wood Street, Now this pub (it used to be called Players snooker club, and is known as this to many residents) stands next to the original police station on King Street which is set back slightly from the road and the bar is beneath the road level.

It appears that the "Tunnel" described above was more than likely the cells for the Police station as we know that less than 200 yards away there was a prison cell dating back 100s of years.

The only tunnels that we can be 100% certain of their existence, are the ones beneath the Westgate Chapel, where there is a labyrinth of tunnels which make up the crypt, these eventually lead to the grounds of the Orangery where the entrance has now been bricked up.

These tunnels are regularly open to visitors but I have yet to take up the opportunity to descend into their depths myself to explore them.

This is a subject that could be debated all day long and as such I will not spend too much time on it, but it is fair to say in conclusion that what we believe to be tunnels may just be cellars, despite the sinister and exciting association with the word "Tunnel", there is no proof of anything untoward taking place in any underground passageways as this is all they were, a simple form of traversing from one place to another without having to go through the streets.

So the simple answer is yes, some tunnels do exist beneath Wakefield's streets, or at least some underground spaces which may lead to other spaces beneath the streets do exist.

12 A LOST TOWER

Pilkington Tower is a little known piece of history from Wakefield, this building, like much of Wakefield's grand buildings, was built of local sandstone. It was a defensive structure with crenellations and it is said to have been built in 1477, we are told that the tower stood somewhere along Dewsbury Road, perhaps between the junction of Waterton Road and Townley Road, although it's exact location is now lost to time.

According to Mr. J.W. Walker:

The tower was demolished in 1724 and the stone was transported into town where it was used to build the West wall surrounding Wakefield Cathedral.

We do not know what became of the stone when the modernization of the Springs pedestrian area was undertaken, it does not appear that the remaining wall standing there is the original stonework from Pilkington Tower, I may be wrong about this but I am certain that someone with more knowledge of dating stonework will be able to confirm if it is of the right period, or not.

It is believed that the tower was a separate

residence to Snapethorpe hall or a possible replacement for the old Snapethorpe Hall which was close by.

So what happened to the stones after the Cathedral wall was removed?

Were they reused for the boundary of the graveyard which stood on the springs on the north side of the Cathedral?

I have investigated, where access is possible, the area which was once the burial ground. There are indeed some very large cut sandstone blocks with many years of weather pitting that remain very close to the side of the old Vicarage, a small expanse of wall opposite the Zetland Street Masons Lodge, these large sandstone blocks are very reminiscent of those which remain at sandal castle but this may just be coincidence or the fact they may have been quarried from the same local quarry, but they could have been remnants of the tower at Lupset.

Could these be from Pilkington tower? Or were the stones used to build another structure in Wakefield? In the 1700s Wood Street was beginning to take shape so perhaps one of the buildings here was erected using the pre carved sandstone blocks? Unless there are records from the period that we have not discovered (or we have not been given access to) then we may never know, but it is not unknown for stone to be reused over the centuries.

We also have to question what happened to the sandstone masonry that made up Wakefield's most famous castle, Sandal, tons of stone disappeared from the towering structure and grand curtain walls which once stood overlooking the river.

If we wander around the village of Sandal it is obvious that there is stonework that was removed from the castle and reused to build some of the houses and a few garden walls or outbuildings.

The castle at Sandal was apparently a structure of gigantic proportion, there would have been a large amount of stone left among the ruins after Cromwell ordered the building to be torn down in 1645, two years after the battle of Wakefield in 1643.

We know that many castles were robbed of their masonry and it is possible that people would come from miles around with carts to take the stone to use in their own builds, so it is also a possibility that the stone from Sandal may have ended up anywhere within the Wakefield district.

One location does give us a very big clue as to where some of the lost stone ended up, St Helens church at Sandal was originally owned by the same gentleman who owned the land at Sandal Castle, I was recently informed of this by a friend who also told me that the church had been rebuilt several times throughout the years and stone from the castle had been used for this.

There is also a large wall to the right of the main gate into St Helens and the stone used to build this looks to have also come from the remains of Sandal Castle.

12 The Origins, of the Bullring.

Anyone who lives in Wakefield knows of the Bullring, the pedestrianized area which stands at the crossroads of Westgate, Northgate, Westmorland Street and Union Street.

Now it has a modern fountain in the Centre where a statue of Queen Victoria once stood proud (the statue has now been removed and re-homed at the top of Rishworth Street), Children play in the fountain while consumers wander past without knowing that this location was once the place where a barbaric "sport" took place.

We know it as part of the old cattle market, but at one time there would have been a large iron ring embedded into a stone in the ground, this would be where a bull was tethered by rope or chain to the ring in its nose and dogs set upon it, while those around watched and gambled on which dog would be tossed into the air and which would bring the bull to the ground.

These were of course specially bred dogs for this ugly "sport", English Bulldogs, and bulls wouldn't have been the only beasts to have been tethered here for this "sport", bears still roamed the woodlands during the medieval period, many of these would have been captured and met the same fate as the bulls had endured.

Wakefield wasn't the only town to divulge in this vicious act, and many towns and cities across England in the medieval period would have taken pleasure in watching the fight between dog, and beast.

Personally I do not see this as sport, but that is what it was seen as in the medieval period, and what may seem barbaric and inhuman to us now, would have been a regular site for visitors to the market of the day.

13 BATTLEFIELD BODIES.

One of the biggest mysteries surrounding Wakefield is the events which took place in the aftermath of the battle of Wakefield, during the Wars of the Roses in 1460.

Historians have long debated as to the full extent of the dead at this battle, but estimations put the toll around 2800, of which only 200 were Lancastrian soldiers.

So, what happened to the remains of those who died at the battle? With such a large amount of fatal casualties at the battle-site, we have to assume that the dead have to be buried somewhere within the vicinity of the site.

It is common belief that much of the battle took place on the park between Manygates lane and Barnsley Road, here the medieval ridge and furrow farming is still visible, however there is no actual documentation, and there have been no archaeological finds to back up the theory that the fighting reached this location.

The only hint we have that any fighting took

place in this location is the Victorian statue which is dedicated to the Duke of York, this stands by the school on Manygates lane, I have given mention to this monument further along in this book but we do know that this is not situated in the spot where Richard actually fell, in fact the only human remains ever discovered in relation to the battle were the afore mentioned Knights, discovered in 1825 by the river.

It has always been a mystery as to what happened to the dead after a large battle as very few graves have ever been discovered at battle-sites

This is because of a few factors, the first being that the topography of the landscape has changed dramatically since the events; land has been built on, farmed, quarried or mined for centuries.

The second factor we must take into consideration, points to most battlefields expanding across vast spaces, thus making it difficult to pinpoint any burial site.

What do the history books inform us about other battles of the period and what happened to the casualties of war during the medieval period?

If you were a wealthy noble and you died in battle, your body would have most likely be laid in a local chapel or church until it was collected by your kin, even wealthy soldiers would have had the option to join a confraternity or parish which would give them the insurance that their body would be collected and returned home.

This option would cost them a weekly subscription, very much like an insurance policy of today, the retrieval of a member of one of these organizations would usually be within a set radius of mileage from the local guild between three and six miles depending upon the policy.

These wealthier soldiers would be given a burial fit for any Christian, even if they could not afford it themselves and as such we have to wonder how many of the dead at the battle of Wakefield were of noble birth or could afford the luxury of being a guild or parish member.

Gregory's Chronicle claims that 2,500 Yorkist's perished, and that as mentioned above only 200 Lancastrians died at the battle. The Yorkist nobles whose deaths were recorded are: Richard (Duke of York), The Earl of Rutland, Richard Neville, Edward Borchier, Sir Henry Radford, Sir James Pickering, Sir Thomas Parre and Sir Thomas Harrington, the latter was killed either during the battle or died of his wounds the following day.

There were eight nobles that died that day, that we are aware of, and Richard was captured and killed at the battle, history tells us that his head was removed and stuck on a pike, this was then mounted on Micklegate in York along with the heads of the Earl of Rutland and Richard Neville the Earl of

Salisbury.

So we know for certain that three Yorkist nobles were removed from the battlefield and decapitated, although we do not know if this took place before or after they were removed from the site, it can only be presumed that remains of the other five nobles were taken home to their respective counties and laid to rest.

This brings us to the big question regarding the battle of Wakefield, what happened to the corpses of those who could not afford the insurance or were not of noble birth?

What became of the simple Archer, the Pikeman or the farmer with his sharpened farming tool?

To begin with, if bodies were left for any amount of time they would begin to decompose, this would cause disease and the obvious bad odors which would drift upon the wind, even if a corpse was left for one night, any dead on the battlefield would have been stripped of weapons, armor and any valuables, often left naked to nature and the elements, it would not take long for Ravens to begin feasting on the dead.

It was not only the opposing side who would strip bodies, chancing locals would have wandered into the aftermath picking up weapons and armor or personal goods at their pleasure, even your own comrades may have robbed you of your worldly possessions if you died on the battle-field.

In an order dated 19th February 1484, King Richard III provided funds to Saxton church and another chapel so that bodies from the battle of Towton could be retrieved and reburied on consecrated ground. The battle of Towton took lace only 24 years after the battle of Wakefield, so can we assume that a similar practice was in place at Wakefield too?

Only a handful of mass graves have been discovered on battle-sites around the country and it appears that even fewer were cremated or burned, the mass grave which was discovered at Towton contained only 37 skeletons, which is a rather small number in comparison to the amount of men who were said to have taken place in the battle, although it is often argued as to how many men took place in this and other battles during the Wars of the Roses.

The shallowness of the grave at Towton is also relative to the season that the battle took place, it was winter and the ground would have been frozen, which would have made it extremely difficult to dig, so with this information we can presume that any mass burials at the battle of Wakefield would have had a similar fate in late December of 1460.

Where do we begin to search for the remains of the combatants? There are very few features of interest in the immediate vicinity of the castle and much of this has been excavated with no human remains discovered, and as I have already mentioned, although castle Park is suggested to be the most obvious of sites for the battle to my knowledge there has been nothing discovered to prove this. As such I would like to put forward a few alternative locations for where the dead may lay.

The modern technology of Lidar gives us a rare insight into how the land may have looked before buildings or even trees were on the land, it shows hills, ditches and anomalies that cannot be seen by the naked eye, when we view the area immediately to the north of the original castle entrance and approximately forty yards south west of Castle Road West there is a faint ring, this is quite a large anomaly, approximately 50 feet across, which looks possibly to be a ring ditch or reminiscent of an Iron age ditched round house.

This could however be a potential mass burial, although I cannot see any reason for a ditch being dug around the site of one, but we cannot rule out the possibilities.

Another area which is rather difficult to determine its origin, is a grassed over location on Portobello Estate, situated directly between Warren Avenue and Clifford View, this area seems to have been undeveloped and consists of a large mound, since writing this I have been informed that this area was used as a rubbish tip for some time, although I am not sure how much credence there is in this claim.

It is more likely that this was created during the building of the estate, and being 750 yards north of the castle, it would have been some distance to carry those men who were killed close to the castle gates. We cannot say that no one died on the doorstep of Sandal castle, and it seems more likely that the fighting took place between there and spread downhill onto the fields where Portobello Estate now stands.

To the south west of the castle is an unusual shaped area that appears fenced or walled off in the old 1800's maps, this area is now under water where a natural pool has appeared throughout the years, but before the water filled it in this was a large depression in a field 480 yards (approx.) below the castle.

This seems to be the second closest possible location for burials, it is only around thirty yards from the old cart track which connects to Castle Road West and Milnthorpe Lane and would have been a good location to lay the remains of many men, it is on flat ground but it is also very close to the area which was once marshland.

We could, however, say the same for much of the other land which belongs to the farm close to this location, to the rear (north west) of the renovated buildings which stand close to the field with the water filled depression, the land looks to be very uneven when viewed on the Lidar map, this could be due to farming or building work or it could be small mounds housing burials.

There are a few more locations around the area of Sandal Castle that look to have "suspicious" mounds or anomalies in their vicinity. The grounds of a house on Castle Terrace is one of these, when viewed on Lidar, a large fifty foot by 60 foot, grassed area appears to have disturbance beneath the soil.

The grounds of Castle Mount Nursing home which stands between Castle Road West and Manygates Lane (now closed) appears to be unusually higher than any other land along Manygates Lane, the Lidar map shows this area as a very rectangular feature standing out among other gardens, this could just be modern landscaping of course but we cannot rule it out.

The final location which could be a very big possibility for the final resting place of those killed is on consecrated ground at St Helen's church at Sandal, to the rear of the church and north of the graveyard is an overgrown area, and when viewed using the Lidar map it reveals an almost circular mound in the top right hand corner.

Could this be the burial? We do know that all casualties would have been buried on consecrated ground, however if you had a priest handy to bless the land (or pit) anywhere could be consecrated and as such we may never actually know where all those bodies lay, I have not had chance to investigate this particular location yet but intend to do so in the near future.

It is quite sad to think that so many souls lost their lives in a battle which is said to have lasted less than thirty minutes, and even sadder to imagine that their remains lay hidden still somewhere around Sandal or Portobello, and that they may never be recovered, but they will never be forgotten.

14 Missing Monuments

In the chapter about the battle of Newlands, in the fourth part of the poem the author suggests that the heroes of Wakefield were carried back to town where they were buried in a "common grave" in a grove of beech trees, a marble obelisk was placed on the site with a golden inscription.

> Near to a solemn lonely grove
> Of beech and polar shade,
> The Heroes made on common grave,
> And there the Knights were laid.
>
> An obelisk of marble stone
> Upraied theron they place,
> Awfully grand full long it stood
> With ornamental grace.
>
> In well-wrought characters of gold,
> Which glittered in the sun,
> The warriors next inscribed thus
> The monumental stone.

If we are to believe the words of this poem then we have to ask what happened to this monument.

And where was the grove of beech trees?

We have two possible locations based on road names and one based on a public house, the first possible location is Beech Avenue on Peacock Estate; however this seems a little far from town and at the opposite side to Newlands which would have meant the bodies were carried through town and not laid to rest there.

The second location seems more plausible as it is very close to the town Centre, Grove road runs between Thornhill Street and lower Kirkgate with Grove street coming off towards Ings Road, the name of the road is the only clue we have here although it is very close to the Quakers grave yard on Thornhill Street, could the Quakers graveyard be the same burial ground? I am unsure what the trees are in this area but there are some very large, old trees here.

The third location would have been perhaps on route back from Newlands into town (depending on the route taken) Belle Vue was home to the Grove public house for many years, standing directly beside Sugar lane cemetery, it is not unheard of old burial grounds being used and expanded throughout the years, and I am quite sure that some of the trees in the graveyard close to Doncaster road, are in fact beech trees.

On the 1800's maps there are two monuments marked in the graveyard, one is still visible close to where the chapel was and the other I have yet to find, perhaps this second monument is in fact the obelisk mentioned in the poem? Or perhaps it is a modern monument dedicated to a family or well off person.

Another monument which disappeared was on the (apparent) original site of the Duke of York's grave, this was torn down during the English Civil War in 1643 and we have no real clues as to where it stood or what happened to the stone from this monument.

We know that it was somewhere in the vicinity, close to where the more recent monument now stands, some sources tell us that it was further up the hill, perhaps the stone still exists, buried among other recycled stone from Sandal Castle which make up the boundary walls of gardens or in some cases the stonework of the buildings themselves.

Not many people know that there was once a statue surrounded by Romanesque pillars, It appears that the statue represented Venus, the Roman goddess of love, a similar image of a statue of Venus shows her wearing the same style toga and her hair tied up, while her body is facing forward her face is facing to the left and her left arm holds the toga over her breasts.

It is unknown when this statue stood in the middle of the duck pond, or when it was removed and to where, this is a large piece and I don't ever recall seeing it in Wakefield museum or any other Yorkshire museum I have visited (of which there are quite a few), so where did she disappear to? When was she taken away from the duck pond and why was she removed?

Perhaps she was stolen? If this was the case I am sure there would be some report in one of the old newspapers and this is not something I or any of my colleagues have come across, maybe the statue was taken to one of the large halls or houses belonging to local gentry, it would be interesting to find out where this beautiful piece of art now stands.

She could even be stood as an extravagant garden ornament somewhere in the city, this and the above missing monuments are just some of the mysteries surrounding Wakefield that I am attempting to solve and by bringing them to the attention of my readers I hope we can shed new light on these age old queries.

15 A lost Hermitage

The information in this book and the overall theme is discovering what has not been written about, although I have touched on subjects that other authors and historians have covered themselves, I hope that thus far I have brought new questions about what we thought we knew.

Breaking away from the theme of the book and not strictly Wakefield, I would like to inform my readers of one of my more recent re-discoveries, a lost place of religious interest and importance.

Few people have heard of Richard Rolle, a 14th century religious writer, hermit and mystic.

Richard was born in the small village of Thornton Le Dale near Pickering in North Yorkshire.

He studied at the University of Oxford until his late teens when he left without graduating to become a hermit it would be the beginning of a long journey for the young master Rolle, He first moved into a house with a Squire, John Dalton in Pickering where he resided for around four years and had his first mystical experience.

The theory that Richard spent his final years in a cave near Hampole comes from three 17th Century manuscripts suggested to be copies of medieval originals and kept at the Sorbonne University in Paris, Ricardus de Hampole admitted to the Sorbonne in 1320, entering the prior's register in 1326, and noting that he died in 1349 among the sisters of Hampole near Doncaster in Yorkshire.

There is some debate among scholars as to the authenticity of the manuscripts and as the only photograph of the suggested cave where Rolle is said to have lived until he died, was taken sometime in the early 20th Century we have to take this information as suggestive and not as factual.

There is a man-made cave near Hampole, within walking distance (around quarter of a mile to half a mile) from Hampole Priory where it is suggested that Rolle would walk to each day to give prayer and help with the chores.

The description given with the photograph is that this structure was discovered in the early 1800s by a quarry owner, immediately recognizing it as something of historical importance he ordered the quarry to be filled and a fence erected around the front of the cave.

Through searching old maps I have managed to pinpoint the quarry that was used in the early 1800s, said to be close to the A638 Doncaster to Wakefield road, and indeed I thought I had discovered the exact location of the cave, now overgrown with ivy and surrounded by a thicket of birch and beech trees, hidden from the eyes of those not searching.

I took several photographs of the "opening" and the surrounding area but it wasn't until a few days later when I was looking through these photographs and comparing them to the original 20th Century image that I realized the hole was not the same, it did appear that there were man-made carved blocks of stone in the walls of this opening.

However, closer inspection revealed that unless it was the original cave which had collapsed, the stone and opening I was looking at was the wrong part of the location, another picture I took was to the left of this opening, a large ivy covered banking with several distinguishing bumps at the summit and Birch trees surrounding it.

I opened the image up in my processing program and superimposed the original 20th century monochrome image over the photograph I had taken, I then slowly faded out the original and to my surprise the shape of the banking matched perfectly, like pieces of a jigsaw fitting together.

It appears that I was looking in the right location but the structure is covered in thick ivy making it impossible to see without clearing the obstruction, unfortunately this may never be possible as exposing the stonework will leave it vulnerable to the elements and possible damage by human interaction, as such this is one mystery that we may never solve totally but I am certain that it is in this location.

Did Richard Rolle live there before it became a quarry or was the cave built for another purpose?

Perhaps it was built by a Shepard to keep him dry from the weather, or maybe it was built by outlaws like Robin Hood, it is said that he and his men operated in this area on the Great North Road which passes by just over 1500 yards from the village of Hampole, perhaps this was one of the many hiding spots in the great forest which would have grown in the area during the medieval period.

What we do know is that the structure itself was not very large, it was probably only around 6-8ft tall and of an unknown depth, however if it was a cell for a religious figure it would have been around 10ft square at most looking at examples of religious cells in places like Kirkstall Abbey.

The hermitage was hand built using tool worked sandstone, as such whoever built it must have had knowledge of stone masonry, and it had an ornate looking archway entrance and was built with the side walls visible, the interior seeping into the banking in darkness.

Steps were apparently built up to the entrance by the quarry owner and a fence put around the location, it must have been an intriguing sight for those lucky enough to set eyes on it and I did find remnants of a very old looking wooden fence close to the banking I photographed.

Epilogue

I appear to have covered almost all of Wakefield's history which took place before 1700 in my first book and this one; this isn't to say that I have solved the mysteries of Wakefield's history, just that I have opened up new questions and theories which we can explore.

I shall continue to investigate areas of our history that are questionable or that I believe have not yet been reported and the discoveries claimed, there will always be something about our history that can be challenged, and this includes my own work.

We shall have to wait to see if some of my theories are correct, once work begins on the HS2 route at Newlands, we should be told if any sign of a battle or a fortified structure is found as there will be archaeological reports, and I for one am looking forward to reading these, I am fully prepared to be proved wrong despite the fact I am quite certain that this battle took place.

This is what I believe being a historian is all about, even though I am an amateur in the eyes of the academic world, it is about solving the mysteries of the past, proving theories with tangible evidence and sharing the information in the hope that it brings new understanding and teaches us things about the past that we did not know.

I hope you have found this book both as informative and entertaining, as I have writing, researching and investigating the content within. I am sure that there may be other mysteries which I have not mentioned, but I felt that I would keep this book focusing on the major historical questions that keep popping up on social media.

OTHER TITLES BY P.A.ROSS:

A HISTORY OF WAKEFIELD

THE QUEST TRILOGY

THE QUEST VOL 1

THE QUEST VOL 2

THE QUEST VOL 3: EMRYS THE TALE OF MERLIN

KNIGHT AT THE MUSEUM

SIR KNIGHT

KNIGHT'S ADVENTURE

UNTOLD TALES

LIFE, LOVE & THE OPEN ROAD

Printed in Great Britain
by Amazon